T0208091

LIFE BEGINS
AT EIGHT

A True Story about a Boy with
No Place to Call Home

Gwyndolin Teney-Rangell

LIFE BEGINS AT EIGHT
A TRUE STORY ABOUT A BOY WITH
NO PLACE TO CALL HOME

iUniverse books may be ordered through booksellers or by contacting:

iUniverse
1663 Liberty Drive
Bloomington, IN 47403
www.iuniverse.com
1-800-Authors (1-800-288-4677)

Because of the dynamic nature of the Internet, any web addresses or links contained in this book may have changed since publication and may no longer be valid. The views expressed in this work are solely those of the author and do not necessarily reflect the views of the publisher, and the publisher hereby disclaims any responsibility for them.

Any people depicted in stock imagery provided by Thinkstock are models, and such images are being used for illustrative purposes only. Certain stock imagery © Thinkstock.

ISBN: 978-1-4917-8072-5 (sc)
ISBN: 978-1-4917-8071-8 (e)

Library of Congress Control Number: 2015918080

Print information available on the last page.

iUniverse rev. date: 11/17/2015

Acknowledgments

This work is dedicated to the memory of Curtis Rangell, my husband, who recalled and shared with me the stories of his humble beginnings. Without these memories, there would have been no book.

My thanks to my many friends who were also anxious to see this story written. Their encouragement has also been a primary factor in determining whether or not this project should be attempted.

A very special thanks goes to Russell Myer who encouraged me to put these anecdotes into a book. He spent many hours reading, suggesting and correcting errors in the manuscript. Also, he generously spent time helping me to maneuver my way around the computer. Without his assistance, this book would probably never been able to reach the printer.

Preface

Life Begins at Eight is a true story of the early childhood of my husband Curtis Rangell. It emphasizes that you can achieve countless goals even when facing inconceivable conditions. It also shows that even with little or no parental guidance one can be decent and honest. Living in situations that are mind boggling, his life while growing up is almost beyond belief.

My husband and I spent many enjoyable hours together while he recalled events of his childhood. It has been a pleasure for me to be able to record these precious anecdotes and the memory his unbelievably adverse upbringing. It is my wish that whoever happens to read this little story will enjoy reading it as much as I have had in writing it.

Shirley Curtis Rangell
fell from the car, breaking his hip
He died the next morning. He was 96 years old.
11/24/1916 - 2/4/2013

Chapter 1

Here I am in the sunset years of my life and looking back, I suddenly realize that I wasn't really born until I was eight years old. My life started out much like it does in most families, but fate had another plan for me. My first few years were spent being coddled by my mother because I was extremely shy. I was a happy youngster but preferred playing by myself. The beginning of my childhood was fairly normal. I had a mother, father and a home. I was like most kids. This was all too abruptly changed when I was eight years old. It would have been impossible to foresee the drastic changes that the future held. This is why I always said that my life began at eight.

Most people I talk to have very early memories. Some people recall as far back as three and four years old. But not me, I am sure I must have played in the dirt like all boys and I do remember how I loved to play with little cars. In those days, nearly every boy had a Durham Tobacco sack filled with marbles. I probably did too. But, so much of those early years, except for a few vague memories, are just beyond recall.

Taken in Roeding Park, Fresno, CA (year 1924)
Jose Maria Rangell, Bertina Rangell, Carl William
Rangell, Shirley Curtis Rangell, Mabel Eva Rangell

In my parents little family, there were three of us children. My sister Edna was the first born. One year later, November 24, 1916, I came along. My brother Carl was three and a half years younger than I. Edna and Carl were both outgoing and made friends easily. They both matured in all ways, earlier than I did.

I was very timid and kept mostly to myself. I do remember that I didn't have any little playmates. I stayed close to my mother who was very protective of me. Because of my immaturity, I didn't start to kindergarten until I was six years old. In every phase of my life, I was slow getting started.

My parents named me Shirley Curtis. They had a good friend whose name was Shirley Browning. I guess they thought Shirley was a beautiful name. Never giving a thought, of how some names might make a boy feel, much to my distress, I became Shirley Browning's namesake. As time passed I realized Shirley, like so many names, can be both masculine and feminine. When I finally went to school, the kids called me "Shirlee-Girlee." This didn't do a thing to boost my self-esteem. Since fighting was not in my nature, I just went along with the humiliation. It was many years later that I finally started using my middle name, Curtis. I could have saved myself a great deal of heartache if I had just changed my name sooner.

I can't recall a whole lot about our house in those early years. It was probably very small. In the 1920s, most houses in little towns looked similar to our house. Ours was built of wood; it had single glass paned windows and no insulation. We had two very small bedrooms, a kitchen where the family took every meal and a parlor to entertain company. We also had a garage for my father's car.

Like our home, in those days, everyone used an outdoor privy. Ours was a "one-holer." It was located out by the garage. There was small grape arbor in the backyard. That was a cool, shady place to play in the summer. When the grapes were ripe, we really had ourselves a great feast.

Since there were no bathrooms in most of the houses, nearly everyone bathed in a wash tub. It was put in the kitchen, and then water had to be heated on the stove and then poured into the tub. This took a lot of time and work, so usually each person only had one bath a week. Not only that, but several of us had to use the same water! Most everyone else in town did the same thing. The rest of the week we had what my mother called a sponge bath. You used a washcloth, soap and a little pan of water. Mother made certain our face, neck and ears were spotless. Since we went barefooted, except when it was cold, we had to be sure our feet were clean before we could get into bed.

We had an ice box out on the back porch. Every week the ice man would come by in his truck to deliver a chunk of ice. There was a pan under the ice box to catch the water as the ice melted. This had to be emptied every day or you had a big mess on the floor. I don't think electric refrigerators had been invented yet. If they had, no one we knew had one. All of the kids would run after the ice truck when it came by. If we were lucky, the ice man would give us an ice sliver. Usually the kids had a scrap of newspaper to wrap around their piece of ice. It was almost as good as ice cream.

A vegetable truck would come around every week. You could hear the vegetable man a block away yelling, "Come look what we have today, fresh tomatoes, turnips, green beans. Bananas, only six pounds for a quarter." All the neighborhood ladies would go out to the street with a pan or box to get vegetables and fruit right from the farm.

Most of what I knew about my immediate family was mainly hear say. My dad told me a lot of stories about his family. How much was true and how much was imagined, I would never know. The sad part is that when you are very young, these things are not important. When I was older, I just never thought to ask about my family. When I was grown and started wondering about my ancestors, there was no one left to ask. Sadly, a lot of what I had been told as a child was forgotten.

I was told that my mother's family, the Fredricksons, emigrated from Norway to Canada. Sometime later, her family moved down to the United States. They settled somewhere in Wisconsin. That is where their daughter, my mother, was born. I never met my grandparents, the Fredricksons. They stayed in Wisconsin for several years before finally returning to Canada. My mother, Mabel Fredrickson, with her sister Ella, and her two brothers Olaf and Pete decided to head for California. They eventually located near Chowchilla. It was in Chowchilla that my mother and father met each other.

My father's grandmother and her young daughter, who would eventually be my grandmother, left Spain crossing the Atlantic Ocean, traveling toward South America. They sailed around the around the horn, up the Pacific Coast to La Paz, Mexico. From there they migrated to California, making their home in the vicinity of El Cajon.

My father's mother, my grandmother, was said to be very beautiful and a very proper Spanish lady. It was in El Cajon that she met and married my grandfather. He was a Portuguese/Mexican by the name of Ranjell (R-a-n-j-e-l-l). For some unknown reason, the teacher where he went to school changed the spelling to Rangell (R-a-n-g-e-l-l).

Grandfather Rangell commuted between El Cajon and Mexico. He was the foreman in a large vineyard, located near the border of California, but in Mexico. It was said that he was well liked, but strange things happen. One day a dispute arose between a couple of the laborers. One worker had a knife and murdered my grandfather. The assailant was never found.

My Grandma and Grandpa Rangell had three children. The oldest boy Ernesto went into the army during World War I. He was never heard from after that. No one knew if he had been killed, or maybe he even married while overseas and just never got in touch with his family. Their second child was a girl, Victoria. Aunt Vick was a kind woman. Everyone loved her. The youngest of the three was my dad, Jose Maria Rangell. He was born in El Cajon.

After my grandfather's death, Grandmother Rangell married again. I never knew her name after she married. I did know that she had several children. There apparently is no record of this part of the family. I was told that when she died, she was buried in El Cajon.

I often wondered why my mother and her brothers chose the little town of Chowchilla when deciding to move to California. There were so many prosperous cities springing up in California. I would have thought that they would have chosen a place like Sacramento where there would be a better chance for employment.

The town of Chowchilla and the river get their names from the Chowchilla (Choushila) Indians who were indigenous to that area. In the early 1900s, a land speculator by the name of Robinson purchased several large parcels of land in Madera County. He subsequently subdivided over half of these into tracts large enough to be suitable for farming. The northeast corner of this large parcel was reserved for the location of the town, Chowchilla. He had the town surveyed, planning for both streets in town as well as many country roads. Robertson Boulevard ran for twelve miles right through the middle of town. It was lined with palm trees, which are still standing today. Robertson then had an office and a hotel constructed. Closely following this, a town water system was installed and his next improvement was street lights.

In October, 1912 a grand opening of the new town of Chowchilla was planned. Announcements and invitations were sent out far and wide. There was to be a celebration with a rodeo and a free barbeque. About four thousand of those invited managed to attend. As it often happens in the Central Valley, the temperature soared. That opening day was hot and dry. To add insult to injury, someone put too much salt in the barbequed beans. Losing interest, most of the "attendees" began to drift away. The little town of Minturn was just 6 miles to the north. Located here was Tom's Saloon. It was like a magnet to those parched throats. Tom did a land-office business on that day. People still laugh and say, that was the day Minturn "went dry".

In 1917, the year after I was born, Chowchilla had become a growing town. Louis Swift, a Chicago meat packer joined Robertson, purchasing the Western

Meat Ranch. It was a parcel of about 40,000 acres. It is an operating cattle ranch to this day. Some time later a "cotton gin" was built. Because of the ideal climate, many farmers had started raising cotton. This industry continues to thrive.

My father eventually traveled north from El Cajon, to Chowchilla. He got a job working for a big ranch. It was here that he learned how to operate all kinds of equipment. This knowledge was invaluable later when his boss went into the paving business. My dad was familiar with, and could operate or repair all the equipment around the farm. When the paving equipment was purchased, it was easy for him to quickly learn to use it. He worked for this same company until he retired.

There in Chowchilla somehow my mother and father met. It is strange how the paths in our lives lead us to certain destinations. It almost seems like there is a master plan for each of us. My mother's family came all of the way from Norway to Minnesota. It was here where my mother was born. Later her parents went back to Canada, and my mother went to Chowchilla. My father made his way from El Cajon to Chowchilla. They met, fell in love and married. My father was twenty-four my mother was just sixteen. This is how my family started.

One day my uncle Pete, Mother's brother, came to visit. He went out back to use the outhouse. A black widow spider bit him on the butt. He yelled, "Help me, help me." My father ran out to see what was wrong. Dad took him to the doctor right away. This particular spider is very poisonous and Uncle Pete was sick for a long time. After that, I was almost afraid to use that privy. I was very cautious when I had to use any outhouse. I learned to have a great respect for spiders, especially black widows.

When I was six, my parents decided it was time for me to start spreading my wings. I had been a mama's boy long enough. The school was located fairly close to our home. Mother took me to school that first day to enroll me in kindergarten. At first she sat at the side of the room with the other mothers. Although I was still shy and somewhat of a loner, I was well behaved and did all of the things the teacher suggested. School was great until I looked around the room. No Mother! I didn't panic, but, I simply walked out and went home. My mother couldn't believe her eyes. "What are you doing home so soon?" she wanted to know.

"I thought you forgot me." She didn't scold, but explained that I must stay at school until they gave us graham crackers and milk. Then, she took me back to school. This time I stayed.

I don't know what caused the fire, but our house burned to the ground. I could never understand why my dad didn't just clean up the burned debris, and stay at the same location. That didn't happen. He brought home an old cook-wagon for us to live in. He had it pulled onto a new lot. This was to be our home. The cook-wagon was similar to the wagons that sheepherders lived in when they were out in the fields tending their sheep. It was very small. It looked much like a covered wagon except it was square. Uncle Pete was now staying with us. He slept on a sofa. I don't know how we were all able to fit in that little cook-wagon. There were five of us plus Uncle Pete. My dad built a lean-to on one side for a bedroom. That helped a lot by giving us more living space. Our lives were very simple then and one did the best they could to survive.

I do remember my mother and dad going out, probably to the movies. They would get a baby sitter to look after us. With our parents gone, we three kids had a ball. We would bounce on the bed seeing who could jump the highest. Yippee! We thought that was great fun. The baby sitter didn't care what we did. Some things like this stand out in my memory, however, most of my recollections of that period in my life are very vague. That was all before I was eight years old.

Curtis, Edna, Carl, Pete Frederickson
(Mabel's brother), Mable and Joseph Rangell

Uncle Olaf was a tall man with red hair. He looked just like the pictures you see of the Vikings. Uncle Pete was also tall. They were both handsome in a rugged sort of way. I was tall and slender. Everyone said I took after my mothers Norwegian side of the family. My sister Edna and my brother Carl were short, stockier and had a darker complexion than mine which resembled the Spanish/Portuguese background.

Uncle Pete and Uncle Olaf were both auto mechanics. Fortunately there was a garage in Chowchilla. They were very lucky to both have steady employment at the same garage.

While we lived in the cook-wagon, Uncle Olaf pitched a tent near us, on our same lot. He and his family lived there for a short time until the house they were building, somewhere else in town, was completed. That house is still standing today, some eighty years later, and looks pretty good.

After Uncle Olaf came to live next to our cook-wagon, he and my aunt would baby-sit us kids when my mom and dad went out. If they wanted to go out on the same evening as my folks, a baby-sitter was hired. Now Uncle Pete and Uncle Olaf both had an eye for the ladies. It wasn't long till that baby-sitter looked pretty good to my Uncle Olaf. Can you believe it; he divorced my aunt and married the baby sitter. I am sure they lived the rest of their lives together. My aunt never remarried.

Across from the Chowchilla City Park, there was a Presbyterian Church. Every Sunday we would get cleaned up and into our best clothes. Mother would take her little brood by the hand and up the street we would go. We liked to go to Sunday school. There were stories, singing and we could color pictures with crayolas. What a treat! My dad was a Catholic, but he didn't pay too much attention to religion. At some point in time, my mother had the three of us baptized into the Presbyterian Church. I think we were very young when this took place.

One day while we were living in the wagon, my mother said she didn't feel well. As the day progressed she became really ill. My uncle went out to the ranch where my dad was working and told him he had better come home. Now! Dad was home in no time at all. He took my mother to the hospital. The doctor explained that it was her gall bladder and that he needed to operate immediately. Dad stayed with her until he was sure she would be all right. She seemed to be doing just fine. The doctor even gave my father a gallstone he had taken from my mother. Dad carried it with him for many years. In the middle of the night, someone came and told my father that my mother had died. She had developed blood poisoning. The year was 1925; my mother was just twenty-six years old. This was before penicillin. That was when I became aware. That was when I was really born. I was in the second grade.

Chapter 2

"Shoo, you kids get outside! Go play!"

Everything was in a turmoil. My mother had died. That meant she was never coming home again. There must have been a funeral, but I don't recall any of that. All I knew was that my life was never going to be the same. My protector was gone and I would have to learn to stand on my own two feet. I don't know how Edna and Carl felt, but I was lost.

My uncles were running to the store to get boxes. I guess Uncle Olaf's wife was helping my dad sort out everything. My mother's things had to be given away. I didn't know it then, but we were moving. Now that he was alone with three small motherless children, my dad was trying to decide the best thing for him to do. There was a lot of "hush-hush" talk. Dad was facing a mountain of bills and had to see that there was someone to take care of his little family. As for us kids, we watched as everything we owned was being packed in boxes. Perhaps by this time Uncle Olaf and his family had moved into their new home, I can't recall. At any rate they didn't offer to take care of us kids. There was only one answer. The three youngsters would have to be moved to Escondido, where they would stay with Dad's sister, Aunt Vick.

I had never been out of Chowchilla. Well, for that matter, neither had my sister and brother. We didn't know Aunt Vick and we had no idea where Escondido was.

It was kind of scary. We watched as the boxes, with our belongings, were loaded into my dad's old car. Everyone hugged us as we were ready to leave. We kids all waved as we left our home. Little did I know that I would never see my uncles again after this last goodbye wave. Many years would pass and I would be an old man before I would once more see the little town of Chowchilla.

My dad's car was far from being new; even so, he had no other way of getting us to Southern California. It was about four hundred miles to Aunt Vick's. This was in 1925 and there were no freeways. In fact, the roads were narrow and not too good. The speed limit was thirty-five miles per hour on the open highways. That meant it would have taken us about twelve hours driving time, to make this trip. With three small children, there had to be many bathroom visits and of course kids were always hungry. Along with stops for gas, we were probably at least two days on the road.

We left Chowchilla and pulled out onto Highway 99. This would be the route we would be traveling all of the way south. There were a lot of farms as far as you could see on both sides of the road. What interested me were the oil wells. The closer to Bakersfield we got, the more we saw. I learned later that in that part of the valley, oil was actually "discovered" in the 1800s. People were aware of pools of surface oil long before the oil wells made their appearance. Wagons would stop at these pools to grease the wagon wheels. Other people even burned that oil seepage for fuel.

Several miles south of Bakersfield were the San Emigdio Mountains. We had to go through the Tejon Pass to get to Southern California. The pass is nearly five thousand feet high. It was quite a chore for the cars to get over that range. Cars had to stop often because their engines would get hot. There was water provided along the way for your radiator. Travel in those days was not for the faint-hearted.

After we finally made it over the "ridge route", as it was called, we dropped down into the San Fernando Valley. I had no idea the world was so big. Now we saw palm trees, lots of orange trees, with oranges, and beautiful flowers everywhere. We were still traveling on Highway 99. "Oh look, there's a lot of water." my sister yelled. Dad told us that was the ocean, and that it went on and on clear to China. Well that was hard to believe! We didn't know where China was, but, that water stretched far beyond what we could see.

At last, we were turning off of Highway 99 and on to the road that would take us to Escondido and Aunt Vick's house. This area was dotted with family farms and vineyards. We saw horses, cows and lots of chickens. We were tired and a little frightened at how our lives were changing so quickly. We didn't know these people where Dad was taking us. I wondered if they would like us. What if they have big scary animals? I'm beginning to feel frightened. Too late! At the end of a long driveway there were a man, a lady, three big boys and a girl, standing by a house waving. We were there.

My aunt and uncle had four children of their own. With three extras, they really had a house full. That didn't make any difference to Aunt Vick. She and my uncle took us in and treated us just like their own family. Carl and I bunked in with their three boys. My sister shared a room with their daughter. This was to be our home for about a year.

Rancho Bernardo (Escondido) was part of the land granted by Mexico to a Captain Joseph Snook. The total grant was about 17,761 acres. Eventually this grant was divided into several large ranches. The town's name, Escondido, comes from the Spanish word, escondido, which means, "hidden". This name was probably chosen, because of the foothills that surrounded the valley. Grapes were one of the most important crops of the valley. There were vineyards all around us. Escondido was quite a farming community at that time. My uncle's farm was part of one of the original ranches. That area is now called Rancho Bernardo. The mild climate was good for almost everything, cattle, sheep, hay, and all kinds of fruit and vegetables. Today the orchards and vineyards are being removed, to make room for housing developments necessary for the expanding population.

My uncle was French-Basque. He spoke very little English. My aunt spoke both English and Spanish. Their kids spoke all three languages. My dad spoke English and Spanish, but we three youngsters spoke only English.

Our food styles varied a lot in my young life. My mother cooked more or less like her Norwegian up-bringing. Here at my aunt's house, meals followed her style of cooking, which was mostly Mexican. We had lots of rice and beans. I remember that my aunt was busy all day long. She spent a lot of her time in the kitchen. She made fresh tortillas every meal. It fascinated me to see her flop those tortillas, back and forth, back and forth, from hand to hand. Aunt Vick was such a nice lady. Every time I think of Aunt Vick, I see those wonderfully kind eyes.

My uncle had a big farm, but grapes was his largest crop. His vineyard was located quite a distance from the farmhouse. It was his pride and joy. Their house sat on a hill. On one side of the hill, below them, was a main road. They had a fruit stand down on the road. My uncle would take a wagon and the team of horses over to the vineyard. He would bring back grapes for us boys to sell at the road-side stand. It was a common thing to see these stands. People would take an evening or Sunday drive to the country to buy produce at them. I got to help my cousins at our fruit stand. We had grapes in small boxes. We kept extra boxes for those who wanted larger amounts of grapes. It was my job to keep the boxes straightened so they were easy to grab when we had a big order.

On the other side of the hill, was where the livestock was kept. My uncle had cows, horses, sheep, pigs and chickens. They also had a garden but I don't know where that was located. There was always plenty to eat. We always had lots of fresh vegetables.

My three boy cousins loved baseball. They were all older than my brother and me, so we weren't included in the big boy's games. After chores were done, they spent most of their spare time practicing batting and catching. They were crazy about baseball. Quite often I could hear my uncle yelling and swearing at them. He swore at them in both French and Spanish for always wasting their time. He couldn't understand why they wanted to spend every minute playing ball. Little did he know that someday all of that practice would pay off in a big way. Those boys eventually became league ball players.

My cousin Pete started out in the minor leagues with the San Francisco Reds. Ultimately he played 2nd base/short stop in the major leagues for the Brooklyn Dodgers and the Pittsburg Pirates. He was probably the most famous athlete Escondido ever produced. He was a nice person, happy and always smiling. He made friends with everyone. Pete was eventually inducted into the Brooklyn Dodgers Hall of Fame. During his eventful playing career, he was known as "The Bounding Basque".

Pete's brother Joe started with the Seattle Rainier's, a minor league. Later he became an infielder for the Boston Braves.

Cousin Steve, the middle boy, was very handsome. He had black curly hair. He was so good looking he could have been a movie star. Steve was a loner and not very friendly. He also started his career in the minor leagues. He played for the Hollywood Stars. Unlike his brothers, Steve never made it into the big leagues.

One day I was outside playing. My girl cousin and I decided to climb up on the roof of the pig pen. The pig pen was behind a shed and completely hidden from the house. All at once she said, "Look what I have." With that said she pulled up her dress and pulled down her panties. I hardly had a chance to get a good look.

Her brother saw her and yelled, "What do you think you are doing?"

Aunt Vick heard the commotion, came out, and was told what was going on. She whaled the tar out of my cousin. My aunt didn't do anything to me. I guess she figured I was too young to know what was what. And that was the truth!

It was while I was in Escondido, that I started in the third grade. The school was about four miles away, so we rode a bus. At school I made friends with another little boy. He had a scooter. It was the kind you stand on with one foot and pump with the other foot. This little boy didn't live far from Aunt Vick's. One day we decided we would ride the scooter home instead of taking the bus. We took turns pumping. It took us a long time to go four miles. It was real late when we got home. I didn't really get in trouble, but my aunt was very worried and made me promise never to do that again.

On Saturday nights, everyone went to town to shop and visit with the neighbors. This was the way of life for many small towns, especially if they were rural by nature. Sometimes we kids would walk to town and my aunt and uncle would come later. They would give each of us kids twenty cents. Ten cents was for the movies and ten cents was for candy. They would visit with their friends until after the show, and then we would all go home together.

My sister didn't get along very well with our aunt. I guess she really wasn't treated very nicely. Maybe my aunt naturally favored her own daughter over my sister. I only know that my sister wasn't too happy at Aunt Vick's. Some lady from the church offered to let my sister stay with her. This solved a lot of problems. Edna lived with this lady for about two years and was overjoyed for the change. This lady liked my sister so much that she wanted to legally adopt her. My dad was very opposed to that; which in a way was too bad. Those two years were probably the best part of my sister's entire life.

Chapter 3

I have no idea where my father spent the year that we were at Aunt Vick's. I am sure he had to return to Chowchilla after he left us. There were a lot of things to take care of pertaining to the death of my mother. I don't know if we owned or rented the lot where we lived in the cook wagon. I guess the ranch where Dad had been working, was sold, because the owner went into the paving business full time. This was the work my dad was doing the next time I saw him.

One day right after school was out for summer vacation; here my father came driving up. My aunt and uncle probably knew he was coming, but nothing was ever said to us. I was surprised to see him. He stayed for a few days with my aunt and uncle. Soon we were told that my brother and I were going to be living with him from then on. I was about nine years old and my brother was just six. Once more there was going to be a big change in the way we were to live.

In the few days that followed, again my clothes and Carl's were put in boxes and packed into Dad's car. I felt a little sad leaving Aunt Vick's family. I had enjoyed the family life we had been living, but I thought it would be nice to be with Dad too. We were loaded into the car, hugs and goodbyes were said. Down the hill and onto the highway we went. "Where are we going?" both Carl and I wanted to know.

"We're on our way to Redlands."

Redlands was a little over a hundred miles from Escondido. It would take us about four hours to get there. We were beginning to get excited about this new venture, so naturally we were both full of childish questions. So many changes had taken place in the last year; little did we know there were many, many more ahead of us.

The red dirt we were seeing as we approached Redlands was probably the reason for the town's name. The main industry in that area was the citrus crop. Redlands is part of what was referred to as the "sun-belt." Its year round mild climate enticed people from the east. Of course the citrus industry drew a lot of people too. For some, it meant year round employment. This was an ideal escape for many who were getting away from the dust bowl areas in the east.

Curtis Rangell and Carl Rangell

We finally reached our destination. Dad said we had a room in a boarding house. We found out that meant we had a room and a lady cooked our meals.

It wasn't a very big room. The three of us stayed together. Dad slept on a small bed, and we two boys had a pallet on the floor. When Dad went to work the next morning, he told us the "boarding house lady" would feed us and watch over us. We had oatmeal for breakfast and bologna sandwiches for lunch. After breakfast she would chase us out of the house, and say, "Now I don't want to catch you out of this yard."

That first day was pretty boring. There was a small park just across the street. After a day or two, the lady let us go over to the park. That was fun. There was a slide, swing, teeter-totter and a sort of a merry-go-round. While we were living at the boarding house, we spent most of every day playing in that park.

In about three weeks, my dad came home and said, "Get your things together, we are leaving in the morning." The paving job in Redlands was finished. We were going about ten miles away to Riverside. It was there that the company had another job.

Riverside was a little larger town than Redlands. However it was a rapidly growing into a big city; the citrus industry was its primary attraction. I don't recall much about Riverside. The one thing that made a big impression on me was that big thirteen hundred foot mountain, right in the middle of town. I never forgot its name, Mt. Rubidoux.

With more and more people arriving, from the east, houses and roads were necessary. My father's boss was quick to make his bid for at least part of the paving work. Here in Riverside most of the workers on my dad's job rented cabins in an auto court. Auto courts were similar to today's motels. The courts differed in that they were separate little cabins. These usually had just one room. In most of the cabins, there was provided some way to cook small meals. In one corner was a bed. My dad bought two folding army cots for us boys to sleep on. You had to furnish your own bedding. Sometimes there were a few dishes and cookware. Other times you had to furnish your own. We were never in any one place very long. This was the start of a Gypsy-like existence. In some ways it reminded me of the story of "Huckleberry Finn."

Like I have said before, Dad worked for a paving company that did roadwork. O.T. Shea was the name of the person who owned the farm in Chowchilla where my dad had worked. He sold the farm, and now Mr. Shea owned this paving company. My dad continued working for Mr. Shea until he sold out to a Mr. Hanrahan. My dad stayed with the company for the rest of his working years. Since the company mainly did roadwork, we went wherever the company had a job. We weren't in Riverside very long. My dad's next job was in Oxnard.

Oxnard like so much of California had once been occupied by Indians. A good share of the state was eventually owned by Mexico. Through a long historical process, California became part of the United States. Henry Oxnard, a Frenchman, was interested in sugar beets. He and his family were instrumentally involved in establishing the sugar beet industry in this area. Eventually the town of Oxnard evolved because of the need for an identifiable place where the sugar beets could be refined. Naturally housing was also needed for the workers so the town grew rather rapidly. During that period in history there was a lot of "wheeling-and dealing" going on in the United States. The land developers were right in the middle of these shenanigans. At any rate, Oxnard became a nice little town. When we arrived, its population was about 5000. The climate was mild and it was very close to the ocean.

Here we rented a little house. Sometimes these places were partly furnished. Sometimes the former tenants just left things they didn't want. What ever was left, we used. Our clothes were always in boxes, so, we never had to unpack or pack very much when time came to move. We didn't carry furniture and a bunch of stuff with us. All we had was our few clothes, bedding and whatever was needed with which to cook, just what we could carry in the car. That was it!

We had just moved into this small house. While my dad was at work, my brother and I explored our new home. We were curious as to whether the former tenants had left anything. We spent the day prowling into every nook and cranny. We crawled up on the sink board to see if there was anything left in the cupboards. Just as we got on the sink board, we looked and there at the window was the landlady peeking in at us. I guess she wanted to see if those two little rascals were tearing up everything while their dad was at work. We were good little kids and wouldn't think of destroying our home. We were just inquisitive.

When Dad left for work each morning, we were left alone. We had to fix food for our own breakfast and lunch. All day we had to entertain ourselves. We played together and if there were any kids close by we probably played with them. On thing, my dad didn't worry about us because we never got into trouble.

Starting in about 1926, the Great Plains, primarily Kansas, Oklahoma and Nebraska, were experiencing terrible dust storms. They were so bad that seeds were even blown right out of the ground. Often farm equipment was buried in a blanket of red dust. People had to resort to wearing face masks in order to breath. Farming was impossible. A great many people lost their property and were literally fleeing for their lives. California with its balmy weather, beckoned to them, so they packed everything they could carry and headed west. Little did those weary travelers realize the hardships that awaited them.

They got jobs as migrant workers. Nearly all were farmers and were unskilled as far as any other type of employment was concerned, so they took jobs following the crops. From Southern California picking oranges, to Central California picking cotton they were glad for any kind of work they could get. On and on they went as far as Washington to pick apples.

My brother and I were not the only children who lived a nomadic life. The children of the migrant workers changed schools as much as my brother and I. They lived in the same kind of cabins that we did or tents as the situation demanded. The only difference was, for the most part, the migrant workers were paid almost starvation wages. With my dad, he had a steady job with a great company and excellent wages. We moved because we had to go with the company. We came in contact with these poor people because they stayed in some of the same auto courts that we did.

After Oxnard, we went on up the coast to Ventura. Here once again we lived in an auto court like in Riverside. Auto courts were not plush at all. Like I said before, there was usually some way to prepare a small meal, but you most often had to furnish your own pots, pans and dishes. Of course we carried our own bedding. The cabins usually had a bed, table and chairs. That was about it. The bathroom was usually an outdoor privy. Auto courts were used by a lot of travelers because they were inexpensive. This was at the beginning of the depression years.

At this Ventura auto court, there was a lady a few cabins down from ours. Her daughter somehow got head lice. I guess this lady thought we were poor and had no mother to care for us; we had to be the source of the lice. When we went out of our cabin, this lady grabbed my brother and me. She examined our hair "with a fine tooth comb". She couldn't find as much as a nit. We told our dad when he came home from work. Boy, he was furious. He hot-footed it down to that lady's cabin and really read her the riot act.

While we were in Oxnard and Ventura, once in a while my dad would take us in the car and we would go for a ride to the beach. The ocean was too far away from our auto court for us to walk. Just imagine all that sand! It felt so good to drag your toes in that warmth. Dad bought each of us boys a bucket and shovel. They were the kind sold primarily for kids to play with while at the beach. We made forts and sand castles from the wet sand. By the time we left the area where there were beaches, we had quite a collection of sea shells. My brother and I even found a few sand dollars. If you break a sand dollar in half, inside are two little angel-like shells. We even chased the little sand crabs. It was so much fun. We didn't have bathing suits, so we never got to go in the water. I don't know if my dad could swim. Maybe he was afraid to let us in that big ocean. We were happy, just to get to play in the sand.

While we were at this auto court, some new people moved in. I guess they were having a feud. They were like "The Hatfields and The McCoys". They sounded like a bunch of banshees; I never heard such yelling, screaming and swearing. They were going after each other with pitchforks, axes, shovels, sticks and anything they could use for a weapon. Thank heavens they didn't have any guns. That bunch was wild and mean. To me their screams were blood-curdling. It is a wonder that no one was seriously hurt or even killed. Someone finally called the sheriff. He came and so did the Highway Patrol. They had a terrible time trying to get that bunch of savages separated and quieted down. I was terrified. We weren't in Ventura very much longer after this incident.

From Ventura we continued on up the coast to South Palo Alto. Dad took us to a campground where you had to furnish your own tent and cooking facilities. Some campgrounds had something like a cement barbeque where you could cook. Most people, like us, had a gasoline camp-stove. This campground wasn't like most of the places we had been. It was poorly organized. There were no camp spaces marked off. Everything was kind of hodge-podge with people camping every which way. We left here immediately and went down to San Mateo.

Chapter 4

San Mateo had what was known as a marine climate. It was greener and had lots of flowers. It was a lot different than Ventura. It was colder and windier than farther south. Also there was a lot of fog. By the time we arrived summer was over and it was time to go back to school. It was here that I started the fourth grade at Beresford School. This was just the first of several schools I would attend while in the fourth grade.

In San Mateo, a Mrs. Sowles had a home with an extra lot within her property. There was a tent that was on a wood floor, located on this extra lot. This is what my dad rented for us. Mrs. Sowles was a great lady. She had five kids still at home so now we had someone with which to play.

On the weekends my dad would pile all of the Sowles kids in the car along with my brother and me.

Five of the Sowles kids and the two of us made seven kids all together. So, with Mrs. Sowles and my dad, the nine of us would go for a ride down the peninsula. That old car was packed to overflowing. Everyone we passed would stare, wave and honk at us as we went by. We could hear them yell, "Look at that guy with all of those kids." I guess they thought, "What a guy! What a big family!"

The Sowles property was out in the country and they had a cow. Every day that cow had to be moved to a spot where there was grass. One of the boys would stake that cow out on a chain. It would eat in a big circle, as far as the chain would allow. The next day it had to be moved to a new grassy area, right there on their property. The Sowles boy didn't mind moving the cow, but I was scared of that animal. It seemed that every time I walked by, that big old cow would look my way and roll its eyes. It had horns too. I was sure that any minute that cow would chase me and hook me with those big horns. Looking back, that poor old milk cow was probably very gentle, but at that time it looked dangerous to me.

We always had our eyes open for a way to make money. There were a lot of acacia trees in that area.

When the acacias were in bloom, we energetically gathered great armloads of blossoms and separated them into bouquets. Then we would take them out to the highway and sell them. We had bouquets for twenty-five cents and some for fifty- cents. People really liked them and we had a big business as long as the trees were in bloom. The flowers were free, so our profit was one hundred percent.

I had one crossed eye. I was lucky, in that none of the kids ever teased me about it. My sight wasn't all that good either, so I usually avoided the scuffles that most little boys have. One day at school another little boy and I were horsing around. We were poking each other and kind of wrestling. We were just having fun. During the scuffle, my shirt got torn. A little girl that had been watching us noticed that I didn't have on an undershirt. She went home and told her mother, "That poor little boy doesn't have any underclothes."

The little girl's mother sent her to school the next day with a package containing two undershirts for me. I was really glad to get them. It was a lot colder here in San Mateo than it was in the southern part of the state. This was also the beginning of winter. Those undershirts would feel really good. I guess it never occurred to my dad, that we needed anything other than underpants.

One of the Sowles' boys got a job at the polo field. He found out that there was a job opening for a flagger. He put in a good word for me. I got the job. When the horses came running down the field, the riders had to hit this little ball. The object was to get the ball between the goal posts at each end of the field. There was a flagger stationed at each goal post. When the rider made a goal, the flagger had to wave a flag that was on a long stick. That signaled that a goal was made. They fired me because I was just too young, and I guess I wasn't too good at the job. They were also afraid I would get in the way of the horses and get hurt. I sure hated to lose that job because it paid four dollars. That was a lot of money to me.

The Sowles family was extremely nice. I really liked living there. But once more we were going to be on the move. Even after we left, the Sowles kids and I remained friends. Many years later, maybe even forty years, when my father died, Mae Sowles, one of the daughters, came to my father's funeral.

We finally left the Soule's property and moved into town, although we are still in San Mateo. Here we rented a little cabin in an auto court. Those cabins were small, only one room, but they were cheap. In this court, there were about eight little cabins. They all faced an alley. We were in and out of this same auto court many times during the year.

I was still in the fourth grade, but at a different school. Now my school is Hayward Park Elementary School. The fourth grade was a disaster for me. We moved so many times. But, my dad had to go where the work was located. Naturally I had to go too. I attended about six different schools while I was in the fourth grade. My dad would come home from work at night. He would say, "All right boys, pick up your grade cards tomorrow, we are moving." Away we would go, another town, another school. My dad never went with us when we enrolled. We checked ourselves in and out of the schools. No questions were ever asked. Moving so much, I don't know how we ever managed to learn anything, but we did.

Chapter 5

From San Mateo we went to Niles. At that time in my life, we didn't move very far. During that whole year my dad's work was in the Bay area.

Niles was a tiny little town at the time when we arrived there. Today it is actually a suburb of Fremont, but it has tried to keep its small town feeling. Everywhere one looked there were references to Charlie Chaplin, the silent film actor. He once lived in Niles. In the early days of motion pictures it was the setting for several of his films, including his most remembered picture, "The Tramp". At one point in time Niles was referred to as "America's First" Hollywood. Niles Canyon was a popular location for a great many motion pictures.

Even though all of my dad's jobs were fairly close, every move was a different school for us boys. It wasn't easy to make friends in such short periods of time. I would just get acquainted and then it was time to move again. That first day that we enrolled in the Niles school a boy came up to me and asked, "You're new aren't you?"

"Yeah, we just moved here."

"My name is Steve, what's yours?"

"Shirley, I'm Shirley Rangell."

"Shirley? That's a girl's name."

I came right back with, "It can be a boys name too, and that's my name."

"Hey Shirl, have you seen the ghost yet?"

"No! And I don't want to see any ghost." I was adamant about that.

"Well, you probably will. Nearly everybody does."

The story of the ghost went something like this, although there are several variations. There was a Miss Lowerey who was riding in a horse drawn carriage and was on her way to her wedding. A horseless carriage, an automobile, came rumbling by. Not being used to all of that noise, the horse was spooked. It panicked and reared resulting in the carriage being overturned. The young lady was thrown from the carriage and onto the road. Just at that time another horseless carriage came by, struck her and killed her.

It is said that she was the first person in that area to be killed by an automobile. Since then numerous people swear they have seen her ghost. Through the years several teams of ghost hunters have visited the area to investigate the tale. The ghost story still persists. She is called the "White Witch" or "The Niles Canyon Ghost".

In Niles, we lived one street off main street. The back of our house was on an alley. Across the alley was a dance hall. Every weekend there was a dance. My brother and I would go out, sit on boxes and listen to the music. The band played lively, toe-tapping tunes. We both loved music, so, this was great entertainment.

When we first moved into this house, I noticed how dirty the back steps were. They were full of grime, dried mud and leaves. I always tried to help my dad keep our places spick and span. Those steps were filthy! I wanted to clean them but didn't have a broom. All I had to use was my cap. I was busy giving those steps a real going over, whacking them with my cap. The neighbor lady came out and yelled, "Hey little boy! What do you think you are doing?"

"Cleaning the steps," I answered.

"You're going to ruin your cap, slapping it around like that," she admonished me. "Don't you have a broom?"

"No, we just moved in."

"Well, young man, you come right over here, I'm going to loan you my broom." What a nice neighbor!

Once when I was going up our steps, I slipped. Down I went! I cut a great big gash in my knee. When my dad came home from work, I showed him what had happened. The cut was so big I thought I should have had stitches. My dad looked at it and said, "Oh it will be all right in a few days." The times my dad ever took us to a doctor were few and far between. I put some mercurochrome on it and it finally healed but, I have a scar on my knee to this day.

In a few weeks it was time for us to collect our report card and move again. Now we were off to Redwood City. Redwood City, like so many California Cities, has an interesting and colorful history.

In the 1920s, the chamber of commerce and the board of realtors sponsored a contest to find a slogan that would be used to publicize Redwood City's finest qualities. The slogan that was chosen stated, "Climate Best By Government Test". A ten dollar prize was given for this brilliant slogan. Before World War I, both Germany and the United States were collecting climate and meteorological data. It was found that Redwood City was at the center of one of the world's best climates. There were actually three areas in this class, Redwood City, the Canary Islands and the Mediterranean Coast of North Africa. When the information of this ideal spot to live hit the newspapers, people flocked to this part of the country.

A deep water channel was discovered that ran inland from San Francisco Bay to Redwood City. It was this discovery that brought the lumbering and shipbuilding industries to this area in the mid-eighteen hundreds. Of the great many ships constructed here, the "Perseverance" was the last wooden ship built in Redwood City and was launched in 1883.

That channel brought many other different kinds of companies to Redwood City. One important industry was a salt brine evaporative plant owned by Leslie Salt Company. During the harvest season, around 50,000 tons of salt are produced daily. This is a very important operation. Salt is used not only for human consumption but also for livestock and in various industries. At the peak of the harvest, the huge salt mounds make an impressive sight as great mountains of salt can be seen from the highway. Leslie Salt Company continues to manufacture a variety of salt related products.

When we arrived in Redwood City, my dad found living quarters for us downtown in a warehouse. There was a creek nearby that we had to cross to get to the school. As usual, we weren't at this school very long. However, while we were in this location, we woke up one morning to find that some stranger had also spent the night in the warehouse. Our dad had gone to work early so we were alone with this fellow. Dad had bought a loaf of raisin bread, so my brother and I decided to make some toast for breakfast. This guy came into where we were fixing our meal and said, "If you will make me some toast, in a little bit I will go down to the store and get you another loaf of bread." We were trusting little kids and believed what he told us. We made him some toast, he ate it, then took off and we never saw him again. He had told us a big fat lie. Before many days, we were on the move again. This time it was just to the outskirts of town but a different school, but as usual we would only be here for a very few weeks.

Next the paving company had a job in San Rafael. Here we camped in a tent that we pitched at some farmer's dairy. We were right across the street from a little one room schoolhouse. There were only about eight kids in the whole school. The teacher asked my brother and me, all kinds of personal questions that had nothing to do with school. I thought she was just being nosey. I didn't tell her very much. It didn't seem to me like she was a very nice teacher.

Nearby there was little creek that ran through the dairy. It meandered in back of the barns, through the field, then across the road and finally to the bay. We had to cross that creek to get to the school. Every day there were a lot of cows that also walked back and forth across that creek. One day after watching those cows, I went home and told my dad, "You know what I saw today?"

"No son, what did you see?"

"I saw a lot of cows peeing in the creek. Dad we drink that water."

"Don't worry about it son, when water runs twenty feet over gravel and rocks, it's purified."

My dad had a lot of peculiar ideas, but at my age I believed anything he told me. We kept drinking that water and never got sick. I can't remember that either my brother or I ever had a cold. If we had any of the childhood diseases, like measles, whooping cough or mumps, it was before my mother died and I just have no memory of it. We were healthy youngsters. About the only time we missed any school days was when we moved.

There was a big field near the dairy farm that was used as a pasture. On weekends, sometimes my dad would hook an old sled to the back of the car. He would pull us boys round and round all over that pasture. We would yell, laugh and have a big time. That was a lot of fun. It was better than a roller-coaster. When he had time, my dad enjoyed playing and entertaining us kids.

From our campsite at the dairy, we traveled to an area that was called Five Points. At this place five roads came together, hence the name. Today everything has changed. Five Points is gone. In its place are freeways, malls and lots of houses. It is now a part of Redwood City. Like so many other places we lived, our time at Five Points was very short.

Next we went back to San Mateo and once again into the little eight unit auto court. We moved in and out of that same auto court four or five times. Each time we lived in a different cabin. While we were there, a fellow who was like a "Peeping Tom" lived in one of the units. This guy liked to spy on the ladies when the sun was just right, so he could look through their dresses and see their legs as they walked. He was married and had kids of his own. I could never understand why he got such a thrill out of looking at the ladies legs. I thought he was a kind of a "weirdo".

Even though my brother was young, he was quite a scrapper. One day at school, some bigger boys were picking on a little kid. My brother stuck up for this youngster and managed to defend him from these bullies. The little boy's father found out how my brother protected his son. He arranged to meet my brother and pleaded with him, "If you will look after my son and keep him safe, I will pay you twenty-five cents a day."

"You bet," Carl agreed. My brother was tickled to death to have such an easy job.

After having changed schools for the sixth time, I finally finished the fourth grade here in San Mateo. The year was 1927. I remember it so well because, this was the same year Charles Lindbergh made his famous solo, non-stop flight across the Atlantic Ocean. He was the first person to be in New York one day, and Paris the next.

Very vivid memories of this next year stand out in my mind. We had to learn fractions! I was in the fifth grade at Hayward Park Elementary School in San Mateo. Fractions were a complete mystery to me. I couldn't seem to understand them at all. I was still too shy to ask any questions. When the teacher would ask me something and I would answer that teacher incorrectly, she would whack me over the knuckles with her pencil. That teacher always had a new, long yellow pencil. She had a deadly aim when she attacked you. I was scared of her. The more she whacked, the more frightened I was, and the less I learned.

One night my father had some friends over to play cards. The lady next door had a boy my same age. He was in my class at school and was having trouble with fractions too. That night, she was going to help her son with his math. "Fractions really aren't so bad. You come over tonight and I'm sure I can help you so you won't have any more trouble." she offered. I thought this was a great opportunity.

I asked my dad, "Our neighbor wants me to come over tonight for a little while, she is going to help us boys with our fractions. Could I go over?"

"No, I want you to stay home." was my dad's answer. I had to sit around all evening watching the grown-ups play cards. Making me stay home was a mystery to me. I could have used all the help I could get.

Very shortly we moved back to Redwood City. The people we rented from had an extra little house behind theirs, so that was where we lived. My dad took me down with him to the P.G. & E. office to get our electricity turned on. As we came out of the office, I was looking up at the sign. "What does P.G.E. mean," I wanted to know.

Right away he came back with, "Pigs Going East." I believed this for a long, long time. I don't know how my dad did it, but he always came up with some very comical sayings.

There was a vacant lot next to us. My brother and I decided it would make an excellent ball diamond. The lot was all covered with weeds. One day we energetically set about clearing spaces for the bases. We also needed a line path between the bases in which to run. That project turned into a lot of sweat and labor. All at once I got the idea that it would be a lot faster if we burned a spot for the bases as well as the line paths in between. We scrounged up paper and matches to get the job done. All was going well until a little breeze came up and the fire got away from us. "Holy-Moly!" Now what were we going to do? A lady passing by saw the fire and called the fire department. They were there in nothing flat and the fire was put out. Those firemen got a hold of us and gave us a good scolding. They told us we would be in big trouble if we didn't find a better way to clear the weeds. They made us promise never to play with fire again.

So much of this coastal region had a lot ponds and rivulets. We were thrilled when we found a small creek nearby. Of course water always attracts little boys and we were no different. We decided it would be fun to make a raft. We were like little beavers gathering up every scrap of wood we could lay our hands on. Finally we decided we had enough. I have no idea where we managed to get a hammer and some nails. Working as fast as we could, we were able to get something built that resembled a raft. There it was, to us it was a thing of beauty, and best of all it floated. We decided it was ready for its maiden voyage. We both climbed on and had a ride. We used poles to push ourselves along. Actually, we thought we were pretty good sailors. In the process of getting on board and off, we got soaking wet. Even our shoes were sopping. We had no idea that, when the leather of your shoes dries after being wet, it gets stiff and cracks. Of course our shoes were ruined and our dad had to get new ones for us. He told us, "To treat you kids good is a crime."

From Redwood City we went back to Niles. The weather had been bad and there had been many rainy days. Of course when it rains the paving work comes to a screeching halt. My dad made good money when he worked. We weren't poor. If the going wage was four dollars a day, he made eight. This was because he could run any kind of road equipment as well as repair most of it. He was a valuable worker. His failing was that he never saved a dime. He lived pay-check to pay-check. With the rain, there was no work, so my dad was a little short of cash. He sent me down to the Purity Grocery Store to ask if we could charge some groceries. I was sure they didn't give credit, but

I went anyway. "My Dad wants to know if we could charge a few groceries just until this rain lets up and his paving work can start up again?" I questioned.

The man at the store shook his head and answered, "I am very sorry but the store policy is, 'no credit'. I can understand your problem young man, but I still have to say 'no'." I went home with the answer I had anticipated. My dad then went to one of his friends. He borrowed ten dollars to get us through this tight spot. At least we didn't go hungry.

At Niles, our class was going on a picnic. All we had to do was to bring our lunch. I was so excited. I wanted to go on that class picnic in the worse way. I could hardly wait until Dad came home so I could get permission to go. We had to bring a note from our parents saying it was all right. When Dad came home I explained all about the outing, and ask if I could go. He told me I had to stay home, and besides we had nothing to fix for a lunch. I was devastated. The next morning I didn't go to school. About time for school to start, sadly I climbed up the little hill that was behind our house. There I could see all of my classmates leaving on the outing. This was near the end of the school year. I don't know when I had ever been so disappointed. To this day it is hard for me to understand the reasoning for some of my dad's decisions.

When school was out for summer vacation, we went over to the town of Herndon. Originally Herndon was named Sycamore Point and was located about nine miles from the city of Fresno. It started as a steamboat landing on the San Joaquin River. Steamboats brought supplies to Fort Miller and later, after the fort was gone, to Millerton. Millerton was once the county seat of Fresno County. One year the San Joaquin River flooded almost wiping out the entire town of Millerton People began to relocate to safer ground. Later in the 1940s, the Friant Dam was built and the town of Millerton was completely inundated by the lake waters. Millerton was gone, but Herdon remained.

When we moved to Herndon we lived in a tank house. My dad was operating a big shovel. He would pick up big loads of dirt with the shovel and then dump the load on to a conveyor belt. There was another fellow down at the end of the conveyor, pushing the dirt into a hole. Nobody knew exactly what happened, but, somehow that fellow slipped and fell into that hole. Before anyone realized what had happened, he was covered with dirt. By the time they were able to get him out, it was too late to save him. My dad was so devastated he couldn't work for several days. The company hired a colored man as a replacement, to help my dad. This new fellow moved into the tank house with us, only he lived upstairs. We liked him a lot.

There were windows in the tank house but they didn't have any screens. We hung our clothes on nails that were pounded in the walls. One night my dad left the window open for fresh air. His good suit was hanging fairly close to the window. Someone came along, stuck their arm through the window. They stole my dad's good suit. We seldom ever lost anything from thievery, but this was one exception.

Chapter 6

My dad's next job was quite a distance to the north, taking us to the town of Navarro in Mendocino County. Actually, it was almost three hundred miles. The colored man went with us. We were glad to have his company. He entertained us with all kinds of funny stories. He was really a good friend to us boys.

At first my dad found a room in a hotel for us. It was similar to a boarding house. We got our meals as well as a room. We didn't stay in this hotel very long. Very shortly my dad located an old shack for us in an abandoned lumber camp. That camp was about three or four miles outside of town. There were several families squatting on this same deserted property. One family was an Indian couple who were newlyweds. We became quite well acquainted with them. We were the only two kids at this campsite.

Navarro at that time was not the thriving lumber town that it had once been. As so many California towns, at its beginning it had a different name. It was originally called Wendling and had been located fourteen miles west at the mouth of the Navarro River. Up at the north fork of the river, a Mr. Wendling founded a lumber mill. Later this mill was purchased by the Navarro Lumber Company and the town was relocated and then renamed Navarro. By the time we came, that mill had been deserted. I don't know why because that area is right in the heart of vast Redwood forests.

Starting the school year, I was eleven years old and beginning the sixth grade. I wouldn't be twelve until the end of November. The school was quite a distance from where we lived, probably three or four miles. We walked to school except when it was raining, and then my dad took us when he went to work.

One time the school was going to have a party. I was so excited. "Let's go home after school so we can get cleaned up," I explained to my brother.

"Nope," was his come back. "I'm staying right here and am going to play with some of the kids until time for the party."

Not me, I had to get spruced up the best I could for something so special. Parties were rare in our lives. So, away for home I went. By the time I had walked home, it was getting late. I was hoping I could get a ride back to town with the Indian couple. They had told me they were planning to drive to the store to do some shopping that evening. I dawdled too long. Before I was quite ready, there they went. Now I would have to walk. It was dusk and before I had gone very far, it was really dark. This was in the middle of the woods where it gets dark early. I walked down the middle of the road. I didn't have a flashlight and I was getting scared. My eyesight wasn't too good, so it made seeing at night very difficult. I just knew that at any minute a bear or a mountain lion was going to jump out and get me. I was sorry I didn't stay at school like my brother Carl did. Anyway, the party was great and I had a good time with the rest of the kids. When the party was over, I was glad that my dad came by the school to take us home so we didn't have to walk through that scary forest. To this day I can still remember how frightened I felt, walking at night through the dense woods.

The Navarro River was close by. My brother and I liked to go to the river to play. The river was only about fifteen feet across. It was cold like melted snow water. It was really freezing but we got used to it. It was in that river that we learned to swim. I can't recall having a bathing suit. I don't know if we went into the water with our clothes on, or if we went skinny dipping. We would wade out a little ways, and then we would paddle like the dickens toward the shore. It wasn't long before we were both swimming like a couple of fish.

Since my dad and my brother both loved the movie pictures, this was our main source of entertainment. As usual on Saturday nights we would pile into the car with about four of our friends from school, and away we would go. My dad had an open-air Chevrolet touring car. This was the only car we had while I was growing up. Ordinarily we kept the top down. When it rained we had to put the top up and fasten on isinglass curtains to keep out the rain. The rest of the time, we took blankets that we would wrap around us. It got cold on the coast, especially at night. The picture show was in Fort Bragg which was fifty miles away. Fifty miles was a long ways in those days.

Also, the road was narrow and crooked. We usually didn't get home till after two o'clock in the morning. That same year the new cars came out with roll up windows. We didn't get one but I'm sure these were a lot better than isinglass and probably much warmer.

One time the three of us were out in the woods just poking around. As it often happens when you are out and about, my dad had to "go". Of course, we never thought to take "paper" with us. Using what was close by, my dad grabbed a handful of leaves with which to wipe. Now those weren't just any old leaves. The bunch he picked turned out to be poison oak. Boy, my dad was in bad shape for a long time. He couldn't work for a week. This taught the father and two young men, to be very careful about the kind of leaves you handle.

We had another short move from Navarro to Philo. This was a little jerk-water town located in Anderson Valley, on the banks of Indian Creek, which flows into the Navarro River. Philo is about ten miles south of Navarro. It, too, was a lumber town. When the company moved, there were several families from the Navarro job that also followed. Arriving at the outskirts of Philo, we just pulled off the road into the woods and found a clearing. Here we pitched our tents and all camped together. My dad carried fold-up cots for us to sleep on. We had a camp stove for cooking our meals. We never cooked on an open fire. It was just too dangerous. The whole area was densely forested. We weren't there very long, in fact not even long enough to enter school.

Philo was just two miles south of Boonville. This part of the country is famous for its apples. There they grew the biggest, juiciest apples that I had ever seen. When you would bite into one, the juice would run down your chin. I haven't had an apple since that could compare with those we found in Boonville. There were a lot of apple orchards around. It wasn't too far for us to walk for a delicious treat.

South Palo Alto was our next destination. Again, here was a city that had once had a different name. Quite a few years before we got there, it had been called Mayfield. In those earlier years, Mayfield was a rip-roaring, rowdy and colorful town. It is said to be one of the oldest communities on the peninsula. The old names seem to be destined for change, so Mayfield, in 1925 became a part of Palo Alto and was referred to as South Palo Alto. The Spanish influence in California is seen in a great many city names. Palo Alto is a Spanish name meaning, tall tree. The Spanish word palo actually means stick. The city was probably so named because of the many tall redwood trees located in that area. The establishment of the city itself owes a great deal to Leland Stanford. It was there that he founded Stanford University in remembrance of his dead son.

We rented a little house that was just two blocks from Mayfield School. At last getting to school was easy. The whole town wasn't very big, not like it is today. There were a lot of stores with interesting names. I will never forget two of the stores I passed all of the time. One was "The Tinker Bell Gift Shop". What a unique name. The other was Madam "Somebody" Fortune Teller.

I was eleven when we got to Palo Alto. My dad would sometimes tell me to take the car and go to town on some errand or other. I would park about two blocks away from downtown and walk the rest of the way to the store. I think letting me drive was just a ruse to get rid of me for a while. He had a girl friend and probably wanted to spend some private time with her. She didn't last too long though. He discovered she was filching change out of his pants pockets. That was the end of that, easy come, easy go. My dad never had any trouble finding a lady friend. We wouldn't any more than get to a town and he would have a date.

At Mayfield School there was a fellow named Lester Steers. He was over six feet tall. He spent most of his spare time "high jumping". He was so good; it helped him finally get a scholarship to college. It is funny how unimportant things like this stand out in your mind after so many years and other memories are beyond recall. I can't remember for sure, but I think I finished the sixth grade here.

Chapter 7

Most of our time was spent in Northern California, but that particular summer the company got a job in Glendale. Southern California was a whole lot different then than it is today. There were orange and lemon trees everywhere. There were big orange and lemon packing houses and Sunkist was a well known California citrus name. Also there were so many walnut groves that there was finally a small town established that was named Walnut. About this same time, people were beginning to plant large avocado orchards. There were great distances between towns. not one town running into another like it is today. Now it is difficult to tell where one town ends and the next one begins. Also there were a lot of empty fields which disappeared with the expansion of the cities.

California had a large population of Japanese. Many of them were born here, owned land and were highly respected. Some had beautiful flower gardens from which they made their living selling flowers. Memorial Day, people would depend on the Japanese for flowers to take to the cemetery. Flowers for Valentine's Day usually came from the Japanese gardens. The Japanese children often kept their teacher's desks ablaze with exquisite blossoms. Other families raised vegetables. If you went for a ride on Sunday or a holiday, it was the custom, to stop at one of their "stands" for produce. Their vegetables were always fresh and very inexpensive. Sadly, with the onset of World War II, everything changed.

When we arrived in Glendale, my dad rented a small house. It sat in the middle of the block with fields filled with wild mustard and what the kids called licorice plants. Once more it was summer vacation for us boys. Since we weren't too far from Escondido, my dad decided it was time to bring my sister back to live with us. She was just thirteen and had been away from us for about two years. She wanted to stay with this church lady where she had been living. The lady also wanted her to stay. She loved my sister and was very good to her. My dad would have no part of it. So her things were packed, stored in the car and we returned to the little house in Glendale.

Foolishly, the first thing my dad did after bringing her home was to dress her like a young lady. He bought her long stockings and high heeled shoes. The dresses he bought were much too old for a thirteen year old girl. This gave the wrong impression to all of the young men. They were like hounds on a rabbit. Naturally they all wanted to meet this new young lady that had just come to town. My dad was furious. He threatened to beat the boys to a pulp unless they stayed away. My sister had been away from us so long, my dad thought he was just being good to her by decking her out in all of this finery. She too, may have gotten the wrong message by being dressed too old for a girl just thirteen.

In Glendale there was a bakery close by our house. Every morning the owner would get rid of all the day old donuts, coffee cakes, sweet rolls and sometimes even pies and cakes. He would put them into a flour barrel out in back of the store. He was always careful how he placed them into the barrel so the pastries didn't get all messed up. Anyone who wanted to could just help himself. As soon as we discovered the "bounty- barrel", we visited the bakery every day. We made sure we got our share. I couldn't believe all the good stuff we found.

What a rude awakening it was for my sister upon joining her family. My dad told her there was washing to be done. This was not an easy job. You had to do the washing in a big tub and use a rub-board. Water had to be heated and carried outside where the tubs were sitting on a wooden bench. One tub was for scrubbing and one tub for rinsing. She had to wring the clothes out by hand and hang them on the back fence. This was a big job for a small thirteen year old girl. I doubt that she ever had to do a laundry. She might have helped, but that was all. She was expected to wash clothes for the four of us. Poor Edna!

Her chores didn't stop there. She had to cook and keep the house clean. We ate a lot of beans which were easy to cook. You just had to keep plenty of water on them. Scorched beans don't taste very good. She probably had helped the lady in Escondido with meals, but this was a big responsibility for a little girl just barely in her teens. Edna was a sweet girl and such a tiny little thing. No matter what she had to do, she never complained. Actually none of us kids did.

When we were growing up you knew better than to find fault, sass or talk back. If you "smarted - off", you were in a lot of trouble. I can't remember, but Carl and I probably gave her a hand with the chores especially if she ask us. We loved our sister.

Clements, CA
Little house on the corner where Curtis' family lived

We weren't in Glendale very long. When the job was finished, back up to the northern part of the state we went. We traveled up Highway 99. The interstate freeway I-5 still had not been built. This time we went to the little town of Clements. Clements is about halfway between Stockton and Sacramento but up in the foothills. It was a quiet, little agricultural town. Many who lived there had farms where stock, grain, orchards and vineyards flourished. When the railroad service came to Clements, it provided warehouses in which to store grain, and close by were corrals for cattle and sheep waiting to be shipped to market. The railroad also provided passenger service until the depot and freight office closed in 1936. With the closure of this service, Clements began a slow decline and it became a less popular place to live.

Our house was right on the corner and not far from the center of town. In the evening we boys would go down to the store where people would gather out in front to visit. A lot of the old men would sit around and play checkers. After watching them for a good many evenings, they asked me if I would like to play. I was only twelve that summer and of course I wanted to, who wouldn't. I was tickled because I thought I was a pretty good checker player. Playing with these guys, I won a lot. It wasn't long till these old men were sorry they had let me in the game. I was beating them all, that was when they began to gang up on me. There would be three or four guys against me suggesting moves. This wasn't fair so I finally quit. All the fun had disappeared out of what was just a game.

The Mokelume River ran along the side of town where we lived. Clements was on a kind of bluff overlooking the river. Down in the bottom land, there was an open air dance hall. My brother and I really loved music. The tunes they were playing were mostly those made popular by the big bands. Music like that was hard to beat. Every night that there was a dance we spent most of that evening on the porch listening to the fun below us. We knew some of the songs and would have our own private sing-a-long.

Clements, CA.
Where Curtis went to play checkers

I recently went to Clements to see what it was like. Today, the grocery store is a bar and the dance hall is gone. The little house we lived in is still there on the corner. Also the warehouse where my dad parked the company truck is right where it was so many years ago. However eighty years makes a lot of difference in a town. Many of the old buildings remain only with different names and new businesses. However Clements is still a small and attractive town.

It soon became time to move again. This time we were headed north up the Sacramento Valley. We would follow State Highway 99. The first notable thing was driving through the city of Sacramento close enough to the state capitol to see the dome on top of the building. For me it was quite a thrill. We had talked about the capitol in school, now I was actually seeing it. History had always fascinated me.

At Sacramento, Highway 99 divided. One part, 99E, went up the east side of the Sacramento River. The other part, 99W, went up the west side of the river. These two highways met again in the small town of Red Bluff. For our destination, we took Highway 99W. We were going to the little town of Corning, ten miles south of Red Bluff. All up the valley there were fields of rice and other grains. We saw lots of orchards. It seemed like almost everything grew in that part of the country. There were many orange groves, peaches, cherries, walnuts and lots of olives. People who lived here were lucky, they could raise almost anything. Corning, where we were going, had several olive processing plants. It was referred to as the Olive Capital of the World. There were also big storage silos where rice was kept after it was harvested.

We rented a little house just south of town. There was no school because, it was still summer vacation. We had a few neighbors within walking distance. It seemed like every one of them had a garden. Every few days, here someone would come with an armload of vegetables from their garden. Some even brought us eggs. They said these were extras and they hated to see things go to waste. We appreciated getting all of that fresh food. There was a lady who even "cured" her own olives. Olives when picked off the trees are extremely bitter. It is quite a process to get them so they are edible. She even brought us a few of the cured ones. They were so good. Never have I tasted an olive like that since then. The people there at Corning were very friendly as well as generous.

A lot of the people around Corning were avid hunters and fishermen. The mountains were very close. You could see Mt. Lassen, a dormant volcano, from almost any point around the valley. During hunting season many could hardly wait to go to the mountains, so they could get their deer. During fishing season, there were plenty of fish to go around. The mountain streams teemed with trout. The little lakes had a variety of fish. But, everyone was excited when the salmon run started. The Sacramento River was just a couple of miles out of town. During salmon season, people would flock to the river to watch the salmon swimming up stream to spawn. When we were in Corning the salmon were plentiful. For those who liked to fish, this was a treasure trove. Several men even brought fish to us and showed us several ways to prepare them. I thought they were delicious.

Just ten or so miles south of Corning was the small town of Orland. Orland had quite a few orange groves. In fact there were so many that it warranted building an orange packing house. The ladies would stand beside a moving belt loaded with oranges. They would pick up an orange, wrap it in a kind of tissue paper, and then place it just so in an orange crate. They got paid so much a box. Before the oranges came to the ladies on this belt, there was another conveyer where the oranges were dumped right after they came in from the orchard. The ladies at the grading belt had to pick out the ones that didn't look too good, the culls, and sort the others according to size. The packers were paid by the size of the oranges they packed. It was quite a procedure. Those culls were put outside in a big bin. Anyone who wanted to could bring containers and take as many culls as they wanted. They were free for the taking. We went down to Orland several times and got free oranges.

The area around Corning was mainly farming. There were a lot of dairies. Some farmers milked as many as fifty cows and some small farms only milked four or five. All were milked by hand. The milk was strained and put into five gallon cans. A truck from one of the big milk companies would pick up the cans and take the milk to a factory to be processed. The trucks would pick up the cans from the big dairies somewhere near the barns. The smaller dairies would put their cans on the edge of the road to be picked up.

Sheep raising was also a big business in and around Corning and Red Bluff. The sheep would be wintered down in the valley near these two towns. When the grass was gone and the weather turned hot, the sheep were moved to the surrounding hills. This move was a sight to behold! Hundreds of sheep were moved right down the middle of the streets. There wasn't a lot of traffic in those days. It was a common sight to see a car approaching a band of sheep and have to stop until the sheepherder could clear a path. He always had several well trained dogs to help him. The herder would whistle a certain whistle, wave his arms in a special way, or both, and the dogs would part those sheep just like Moses parting the Red Sea. The car would slowly drive through the sheep. As soon as the car was through, the dogs would bunch the sheep together again, and down the road they would go. Those dogs were a valuable asset to the herders.

One day while my dad was at work, I got a toothache. It really hurt. I stood it as long as I could, then I decided I had to do something about it. I walked, maybe a half a mile to town. I went along the main street looking at the names on all of the buildings. Then I saw it, a sign that said there was a dentist upstairs over one of the stores. I went up the stairs and into the office as bold as brass. This was most unusual for me because of my shyness. The dentist asked what he could do for me.

"Doctor, my tooth is hurting something awful. It is so bad I couldn't wait to get it fixed until my dad came home from work."

"Come here son; let's take a look at it."

"If you can fix my tooth, my dad will come in after work and pay you."

"You climb right up here in this chair. The important thing is to take care of that bad tooth." Again I assured him that my dad would pay him. That night my dad did go in and paid the bill. I was thankful that dentist was so trusting. Things were very simple in those days.

One day we two boys were playing in the field by the house. There were a lot of bushes around. Carl was poking around under some of the bushes like kids do. He yelled, "Hey, look what I found." Wrapped up in some old rags there was a gun and some bullets. It was a 410 pistol with a short barrel. The shells looked like shotgun shells, they were long and skinny. I'm surprised my dad let us keep it. One morning we ask Dad if we could take the gun that afternoon and go hunting. I don't know how we learned to shoot that gun. Dad said it was all right. He added, "Meet me over on Rawson road and I will pick you up and give you a ride home."

That afternoon we walked down the creek bed and out through the fields. We never even gave a thought about snakes. Today, I think it was a miracle we didn't run into a rattler because those dry fields were considered rattle snake country. On this adventure we actually shot a rabbit. After we skinned and gutted it, we built a fire, put that rabbit on a stick and roasted it. Boy, that rabbit smelled so good! We divided it up, but when we started to eat, we remembered we hadn't brought any salt. That was one flat tasting rabbit. It wasn't long till we realized we hadn't brought any water either. Summers in Corning are hot and this day was no exception. Sweat began to run down our faces and the middle of our backs. Before long it felt as though our tongues were hanging out and our mouth seemed full of cotton. We had never heard about putting a stone in your mouth to help ease your thirst. By the time our dad arrived to pick us up, we thought we were about ready to die.

Once a couple of the neighbor's kids came over, we were just fooling around when one of them asked, "Are you going to go to school with us here in Corning?"

"My dad hasn't told us what we are going to do yet. I think we will probably go back to the Bay area before too long."

"How come?"

"Well, school starts the first of September and my dad's work here, won't last very long, so I think we might be moving soon."

"We don't start school here until after the prune harvest."

"That's a funny way for school to start." I laughed.

"No," he argued. "Everybody helps in picking prunes. The schools understand that the guys who have the orchards need workers. Besides, most of our families, kids and all like to make a little extra money. We can't be in two places at once so the schools just wait to start until the harvest is over."

"Do you have to climb a ladder to pick prunes?"

"Nah, the trees aren't that big. You just take a big tarpaulin, spread it under the tree. Then you smack the tree limbs with a stick. The prunes fall off and then all you have to do is pick them off the canvas and scoop them into boxes. We get paid so much a box. My mom and all us kids work in the prunes. We take a picnic lunch and work all day. It's 'kinda' fun."

"How long does it take? When do you start to school?"

"Oh the harvest is over in a couple of weeks. We start to school around the middle of September."

"It sounds like a neat way to make money, but I'm sure we will be gone, long before the prunes are ready to pick."

Chapter 8

In Corning, our company hired a grease monkey to keep the crane and other equipment in good working order. We got well acquainted with his whole big family. Nearby, one of the large rice growers provided a bunk house for its field hands and included meals. The grease monkey's mother cooked for this group of workers that labored in the rice fields. Little did I know that this grease monkey and his mother were destined to eventually bring about many drastic changes in my life.

When we left Corning, it was back to the Bay area once more. This time we went to San Mateo. It was just in time for me to start in the seventh grade. That fellow, who was the grease monkey, went along with us. He continued to work for the company for a long time.

In San Mateo we once more had a place in that eight unit auto court where we had lived so many times. The owner, Mr. Heckenkemper, was a great guy. Every time we would come back, he would find a place for us. We called this "Heckenkemper's Alley". In the alley, up towards the front, there was a little grocery store owned by the Swyteks. The Swyteks had a little boy that we liked to tease. We would get him down and tell him we were never going to let him up. He believed us, and he was scared. My brother and I didn't mean any harm; in fact we were just having fun teasing him. Now I realize that what is fun for one person isn't necessarily fun for the other person.

One day, I went to my father and said, "Dad I need to talk to you about something private."

"All right son, nows a good time, we're all alone."

"Well", I hesitated, "I smell bad … … down there."

"Pull your pants down. I need to take a look so I can see what your trouble is." I was really embarrassed to expose myself, but I did what he asked. "Oh son, you have to take better care of yourself. 'That' has to be kept very clean." He then explained exactly what

I needed to do. I felt better just knowing there wasn't anything seriously wrong with me. All went well for a couple of weeks. Then, one day Dad came in and told us boys to get cleaned up, we were going to town.

Hooray! Going to town usually meant shopping or the movies. We hurried and were ready in no time at all. We jumped into the car and away we went. When we got into town, Dad pulled up in front of this professional building. He didn't tell us anything. One seldom knew what was going on in his mind. We went with him into this medical office. In just a few minutes we boys were taken back into a room. By the time we figured out what was going to happen, it was too late. That day our dad had us both circumcised. We thought our manhood had been mutilated. This is a painful surgery. The recovery was especially painful for young boys who are just entering puberty.

That year I was back in Hayward Elementary School. I stayed in this school through the eighth grade. My eighth grade teacher was Mrs. Clifford. She was such a nice lady. Often when she had errands to run, she would ask me if I would like to ride along. I thought this was great. She somehow knew that my life wasn't like the average youngster in her class. When it came time for graduation, she offered to drive me to the high school auditorium where the graduation exercises were held.

At this point in time our sister was still with us. I don't think she was ever happy after she left Escondido. Being the oldest, and a girl, my dad expected her to cook, do the washing and any cleaning necessary. She became almost a slave for the rest of us. One thing about my sister, she didn't grumble because of her many chores. It seemed to me like her work was never finished. I don't know how she managed. When school was in session, my dad also expected her to go to school. She missed a lot because she wasn't very interested. I imagine, often she was just too tired to go. She finally quit school before she graduated from the eighth grade. That grease monkey, who was working for my dad and who had come with us from Corning, he and my sister were sweet on each other. When she was fifteen and he was eighteen, they got married. After she married she moved away only to continue the rest of her existence in drudgery. I rarely saw her after that. She and the grease monkey had a boy and a girl before she divorced him and remarried. She had another boy and a girl in her second marriage. It seemed to me as though she didn't pay too much attention to her children. I wouldn't see her for months at a time and then all at once she would show up, and then disappear again. She never had a happy life.

I had no more than started high school when we moved to Santa Margarita. We camped out down in a creek bed. My brother and my dad slept in a tent. There was no way I was going to sleep in there with them. I just knew that there were bugs, snakes and all kinds of varmints that might get me. I am fourteen years old and still afraid of my shadow. I got busy with a few boards that I managed to locate, and made myself a bed in a tree. No one ever told me that snakes could climb trees. I thought I was really safe. The high school was in Atascadero which was about six miles away, so in order to get to school I had to catch the school bus. I hardly had time to find my classes and get to know a few of the kids, before it was time to move again. We were only there about three or four weeks.

Our next stop was Redwood City. Right away, my dad got acquainted with a Mexican lady who had two grown kids. He told her he was looking for a place to stay. She said she had an extra room at her house that she would be willing to let us rent. My dad was happy about this, and she let us move right in. My dad wasn't sweet on her or anything like that. It was just a place to stay, and it meant an extra dollar or two for her. One night he asked her if she would like to go for a little ride, and she was eager to get away from the house for a couple of hours. Before they left, my dad had gone down to the bakery and bought a cake. It was a big chocolate cake with gooey looking frosting. They took off for their ride and that cake was left sitting on the table. I couldn't keep my eyes off that beautiful masterpiece. It looked so yummy! My brother told me, "I'll cut you a piece of cake if you want me to."

"Oh no", we wouldn't dare," was my reply. "Dad would just about kill us." Well my brother was more daring and braver than I. He got a knife and cut me a great big piece. Of course, I ate it. That was the best cake I ever tasted. It was worth every bit of the "dressing down" we were going to get from my dad. I was really surprised when he never said a word about that missing piece of cake.

During the couple of months that I went to Redwood City High School, I signed up for baseball. I couldn't see worth a darn. I had that one crossed eye and I couldn't see too well out of other eye. In spite of this handicap, I still wanted to play baseball. One afternoon at practice, I was up to bat. The ball was pitched and came flying toward me. I put my arms and the bat up ready to hit it. That ball was coming at the speed of light. I missed the ball, but it didn't miss me. It hit my arm just above the wrist. My arm hurt like the dickens, so, I went home. Our neighbor took me to the doctor. X rays were taken; they told me my arm was broken. The next day I reported it to the school. It was too late. Now, the school insurance wouldn't do anything about paying for it. They said I could have just as easily broken it at home. I should have reported it to the school office right when it happened. That was one of many lessons I learned the hard way.

Next door to our house there was a cigar store. The man who owned it didn't have any legs. He was always in a wheelchair. I spent a lot of time with him. He told me all kinds of stories about the early days. I enjoyed listening to all of those wild tales. He treated me like I was his own son. Just about every week, a nice car would pull up in front of the store. This very pretty lady would get out and go into the store. The two of them then, would go into his house and shut the door. In about an hour she would come back out, get into the car and drive away. In a few minutes the cigar man would come out looking please as punch. I didn't know what happened, but whatever it was, it made him very happy.

We just lived with this Mexican family for maybe a month or six weeks. I never cared for the lady. In fact, she looked sneaky to me and I didn't trust her. I don't know why I felt this way. She was always very nice to us. In spite of that, I was still glad when we moved from her house.

Chapter 9

`When the short paving job was finished in Redwood City, back to San Mateo we went. The same little auto court had a cabin for us. I was only in San Mateo High School for a couple of months when it was time to move again. This time we moved to South San Francisco. This was to be the last move I was to make during my years in high school.

Early one Saturday morning, my dad told us to get our things together because we were moving. In South San Francisco the company had a big construction yard near a creek bed. This is where my dad drove us that Saturday morning. He got out of the car, looked around and told us we were going to build a cabin here. He set us boys to work gathering scrap lumber from all around the construction yard. We found a lot of two by fours, some planks and anything we thought our dad could use. While we were doing this, he was laying out a plan for our cabin. This was exciting and really a lot of fun for us, looking all over the place and seeing what materials we could find. We helped hold boards while he hammered and did a lot of fetching and carrying. It wasn't long till a floor was laid and the studding was up. Close by there was a railroad siding that had served the construction site. There were several old boxcars on that siding. The boxcars hadn't been used in a long time. We discovered that there were a lot of sheets of plywood laying around in those cars. That was just the thing we needed for our cabins outside walls. It took quite a while for us to get those big sheets of plywood out of the cars and carry them down to our cabin. When night time came, we camped out on the floor of our new home. The next morning, we had a makeshift breakfast and went to work. Dad got the siding up and the roof in place. We even found some tar paper to put on the roof and the sides to keep the weather out. Our cabin was small, about twelve feet by fourteen feet, but it was great as far as we were concerned. It was big enough for our three cots, a small table and three chairs. What more did we need! We had never had much more than this before. Dad built the cabin close enough to the construction site so he could tap into their water supply and electricity. It was great because it was OK with the company and it was free. In our search for materials, we even found an old sink and a lot of old pipe. This sink was a great addition to the inside of our cabin. Dad also made a low square frame and filled it with sand. He got an empty oil drum, welded an opening with a little door through which to put wood. This made a great stove that served for both cooking and heat. We bathed in a wash tub and built a "one-holer" about fifty feet from the cabin. There were a lot of willows growing in that creek bed, so we said that we lived in "The Willows". Dad must have had some long term plan in mind, because never have we had anything so permanent since I was eight years old, and lived in Chowchilla. Once more he never gave us a clue regarding his intentions.

Now that my sister had gone, my dad took over the job of cooking. He fixed pretty good meals. We had meat, potatoes and vegetables. Of course, we always had plenty of beans. For dessert, there was always bread and strawberry jam. When Dad would leave for work, if we were having beans, he would caution us,

"Be sure you boys keep plenty of water on those beans. I don't want them to burn." We remembered most of the time but when we forgot, and the beans scorched, they tasted awful and we got scolded.

Dad replaced our old fold-up army cots with metal cots that had mattresses. These were a lot more comfortable. Now that we had a wood stove we didn't use the camp stove any longer, but my dad kept it for future use. This cabin was to be my home for the next four years.

I was still a freshman by the time we located in "South City". I had changed schools so many times the school told me I was going to have to repeat my freshman year. I was way behind everyone else in the class. I understood, and it was OK with me. I liked school and was glad that we would be able to stay full time in one place.

It wasn't but a week or two, till Dad left us two boys alone to finish out the few weeks remaining in the school year. Never before were we left completely alone. I was in the ninth grade and Carl was just in the sixth. It was kind of scary.

The company sent Dad over to Delevan, a little community about forty miles south of Corning. It was located in Colusa County and was so small it didn't even have a post office. There are a lot of fairly large farms in the vicinity, but the main interest was the Delevan National Wildlife Refuge.

This refuge can be visited via a one-way dirt road that winds around, skirting multiple pools and swamps. Scattered through-out, are viewing platforms for taking photos or just observing. Huge flocks of ducks, geese, swans and other migratory birds, either rest here or winter over. One might also see beaver, muskrats or an occasional deer. A person never knows what will be seen, but seldom is a visitor disappointed. It is well worth a visit.

After arriving at Delevan, I guess work got short for a little while. In order to keep my dad busy, the company wanted him to paint all of the equipment at this job site. This was great as far as my dad was concerned. He looked around and found a lot of black shiny paint. It wasn't but a few days till he had everything looking spiffy. Then the boss dropped by. "Joe, I hate to tell you this after all of your work, but the state law says all equipment has to be painted yellow." Of course that was kind of a low blow, but my dad just took it in his stride and repainted everything yellow.

As soon as school was out, Dad came back to "South City", picked us up and took us to Delevan to be with him for the summer. He just put a padlock on the door of our cabin and left everything. I was now fifteen years old. At Delevan, we lived in a scale house right on the job site. A scale house is part of the area where trucks carrying grain or cattle were weighed.

There was a family across the road and down a ways that had some kids. My brother and I became friends with them. The kid's parents had a "Big Orange" stand out in front of their house which faced Highway 99W. They sold fresh orange juice. All over California there used to be a lot of these stands shaped like oranges or lemons. That was a time before any freeways, so 99W was a main artery between Sacramento and Red Bluff. Business was very good, especially in the summer, because the summers in this part of the country are very hot, often exceeding one hundred degrees. Thirsty travelers found these stands welcome and refreshing. The big house where our friends lived is still standing today, but, the Big Orange has been gone for a good many years.

Irrigation Direct
Where boys went to swimming & barn
where they changed clothes

Carl and I chummed around with these boys all summer. There was a big irrigation ditch within walking distance, so we spent a lot of time swimming. There was a big tin barn right next to the irrigation ditch. The farmer who owned it told us we could change clothes in there. He cautioned us to be sure to shake our clothes good before putting them on, because a black widow spider might decide to crawl in them and I knew plenty about those black widows. One day, I dove in the water and hit my head, especially my nose. I most likely hit it on a chunk of cement. I really hurt my nose. I thought I had probably broken it because it was all shoved over to one side. My dad said not to worry that I would be all right. Kids were tough in those days, they had to be, and my dad didn't believe in always running to a doctor. I survived but I probably should have had stitches and maybe even a tetanus shot. It was years later, after I was grown, that I finally got my nose straightened.

As I have said before, the movies were my dad's big thing for entertainment. Often, early Saturday morning, he would say, "Have your friends get a dime and be here at six tonight and we'll all go to the picture show." The closest picture show was either at Willows or Orland. I can't remember which. That would make it thirty or forty miles north of Delevan. The kids who lived close by were tickled for the chance to get to go with us. Their parents trusted my dad, so we generally had a car full.

One time, there had been an accident out on the highway. After the police had everything cleared away, an insurance agent showed up. He was talking to my dad to see if he knew anything about what had happened. He needed a drawing showing the position of the cars and all the other details as to what had taken place. Dad, always proud of his boys, offered, "My oldest son has had mechanical drawing in school. He is great and would be glad to draw this out to scale." The insurance man was thankful for a chance to have some help. He came right over to me and explained what he needed.

"I'm just a beginner and this would be more than I know how to do," I declined. Maybe I could have helped the guy out, but I was just too reticent to even try.

When summer was over we all went back to South San Francisco. In the meantime, the company had arranged for a job down in the desert near Indio. They wanted my dad to go down there. The work in Indio had something to do with the building of the California Aqueduct. In 1925, the voters in the towns around Los Angeles voted a huge bond to construct an aqueduct to bring much needed water from the Colorado River to Los Angeles. It was to be about a ten-year project. With the hiring of so many workers, the small desert towns flourished. Since this job was supposed to last for several years with no moving around, my dad thought this was a great opportunity.

During the past few months, I guess my dad had kept in touch with the family that we had been friends with in Corning. The lady in that family was the mother of the grease monkey who had married my sister. The mother and my dad got together somehow and were married. She had quite an extended family of seven. When my dad married her, he married the whole family. Now he had quite a responsibility. He had to support his new family as well as us boys. Dad took off for the desert with his new family, abandoning us to take care of ourselves.

Chapter 10

I guess my dad had something like this in mind when he decided to build the little shack in "The Willows". However, he didn't leave us destitute. He had seen to it that we had a roof, of sorts, over our heads. We had no water or electricity to pay. The company furnished those. He made arrangements with a store close by for us to charge whatever groceries we needed. The grocer would send him the bill, which he paid faithfully. Anything else we wanted or needed, we had to find a way to pay for it ourselves. We had no refrigeration but dad had built a little cupboard into one of the walls. The back was screened and faced the outside. The side facing inside was covered with a little curtain. This makeshift cooler helped to keep some things fresh. We kept our bread there. It wasn't very good for keeping milk or butter. We managed not to have any leftovers so we didn't have a storage problem or a lot of bugs. We bought just what we needed and no more. Being kids, one would think they would go hog-wild with no supervision. Not us! At the store we never bought candy and a bunch of junk. Like I mentioned before, we were well behaved kids. In all the time we were alone, we never got into trouble. I guess it seemed all right to my dad for us to be left by ourselves. We just took it in our stride like we did with everything else in our lives. Today, leaving two youngsters by themselves, weeks and months on end, would have never been permitted.

By now, summer was over and it was time for school to begin. I had to start my freshman year over. From this time on, I don't think I ever missed a single day of school. I loved school, studied hard and made good grades. Not only did we go to school, but we had to do our own laundry, cooking and cleaning. It took a while to get used to doing everything for ourselves but we did it. We learned to fix simple meals and took pride in keeping our humble dwelling clean.

South San Francisco wasn't always the greatest place to live. It was foggy most every day. Just the way the land lay, the fog would roll right in and hang there. One could look south toward San Mateo and Burlingame, there the sun would be shining, while we were "socked-in". Also, it seemed as though the wind was always blowing. There were very few beautiful sunshiny days.

There was a hobo camp on the other side of the big grove of willows where we lived. There were always a few men over there. They minded their own business, and we minded ours. Sometimes, we could smell the food they were cooking over an open campfire. It smelled pretty good. The hobos would sleep there, and then some of them would move on while others stayed a few days. I think there was a little bridge near their camp. When it rained or was real foggy they could get under it and have protection from the weather. They never came around our place and we stayed away from theirs. Since I always seemed afraid of everything, I am surprised I wasn't afraid of those hobos.

It was so crowded in our little cabin I decided to do something about it. I poked around in those old boxcars and found enough plywood to build a bedroom onto the side of the shack. I really didn't know what I was doing. There was a fellow up at the company yard, so I asked him a lot of questions.

I guess he could see that I was quite a novice when it came to construction. He gave me a few pointers, and then decided to actually give me a hand. With me as his helper, that room was completed in no time, and was a great success. We moved our cots in this new room. What a difference! Now we had room to breath. Carl and I managed to put up some shelves and found some boxes we could stack for a cupboard. We pounded nails in our bedroom wall to hang part of our clothes. The rest of our clothes we put on the shelves we built. We didn't have much of a wardrobe so very little storage space was needed.

Even though our groceries were taken care of by our dad, money was needed for other things. We had to buy some school supplies, a very few items of clothing and we had to have money for transportation. If we couldn't walk to wherever we wanted to go, we had to take a streetcar. So, whatever extra money we needed, we had to get for ourselves. We got a job selling newspapers. My brother took one area to sell his papers and I would take another. We got two cents for each one we sold. We had to sell a lot of papers to make very much. It was a good thing clothes were cheap. Most of the clothes we had came from the Goodwill Store. We knew about buying there because that was where our dad shopped. As long as we were selling papers, our streetcar fare was free. That was a big help.

We also went up to the golf course and put our name in for being a caddy. There were a lot of kids trying to make a little money there. You had to sign in, and then you would stand around and wait for your name to be called. After they got to know my brother and me, they saw that we got to go out caddying quite often. The money we made there was better than selling newspapers as long as they called your name for that day. We got to meet a lot of very good golfers and we even became interested in the game. I enjoyed golf but was never very good, but my brother became an expert.

We noticed that sometimes cars would come down into the creek bed by our house. This creek was actually part of the company's property. We didn't know where those cars were going, or why they would be in the creek bed, but they most often got stuck. Being enterprising youngsters, we saw this as a chance to earn some money. We went scavenger hunting again up in the company's yard. We gathered up old boards that might fit nicely under a tire. We found a bunch of old gunny sacks which would be good for traction and anything else we thought we might use. We stacked all of our materials by our shack. Now we were ready. If a car got stuck, we could offer our help and hope the owner would be grateful enough to reward us. It didn't take long till we heard wheels spinning in the sand. Out we went. "Hey mister, could you use a little bit of help?" we would offer.

"You bet!" was nearly always the answer. Out we would come with all of our ammunition. Under the car we would go placing our boards and sacks, just so, to give the wheels needed traction. Before long, out that car would come. The car owners were always so grateful for our help, that they usually gave us a dollar or more. After each "rescue" job, we would then gather up our stuff, stack it and wait for the next "stuckee."

On Saturdays the big thing for me, was to go to the library. I would spend all day there. I loved to read. I can't understand why today, the libraries are closed on Saturdays. This is the time kids have a chance to go and really get acquainted with all of the treasures that are in those wonderful books. I would rather see them closed one day in the middle of the week, but for the children's sake, never on Saturday.

Sundays were my worse day. There was no school and no library. However, sometimes I would go for a hike. The problem was, to figure how far I could go and still get back in time for something to eat. It never occurred to me to pack a lunch.

It was about five or six miles in to school. We walked most of the time. A dime for the streetcar was just too hard to come by. We had to save up so we had extra dimes in case it rained. For lunch, my brother and I would go to a store that was close to the school. We would buy a loaf of French Bread, slice it down the middle, and then cut it in half. On it we would put lunch meat, cheese or whatever we decided. We would each get a quart of chocolate milk. This didn't cost much in the thirties and it was a good lunch for two growing boys. Sometimes we might treat ourselves to an apple or some other kind of fruit. We never bought cookies, candy or sodas. It just never occurred to us.

One thing that puzzles me to this day is that all of the time we were in grade school as well as in high school, no one ever asked us about ourselves. They didn't know our address, actually we didn't have one. I wonder what they would have said if we had told them, "We live in 'The willows'." The schools didn't know where we lived or who our parents were. They never asked. We just showed up for school and that was all there was to it. I guess in grade school our dad might have signed our report cards. I'm not even sure about that. We checked ourselves in and out of whatever school we attended. Dad was gone when we were in high school, so I guess they just overlooked hearing from our parent. To my knowledge they never knew that we were just two youngsters living alone in more primitive conditions than they could have ever imagined. Today, the authorities would never tolerate two children living as we did with no adult supervision. My dad would be in a lot of trouble and we would be in foster homes. But, for us, at that time in our lives, we were better off where we were. We were happy, we didn't bother anybody and we never got into any kind of trouble. One more thing that is puzzling, my brother and I never thought about birthdays, Christmas or any other holiday. I guess they were just another day for us.

I was sixteen when I started my sophomore year. This was a very eventful year for me. One day at home Carl was practicing his swings with a golf club. I have no idea where he got that club, unless someone over at the golf course gave it to him. I wasn't paying any attention to what he was doing. I walked right up in back of him just as he started a swing. I was too close and that club hit me right in the mouth. It wrought havoc with my mouth, and my front tooth was broken. Carl felt terrible, but it wasn't his fault. I should have been paying closer attention. When I saved up part of the cost, I went to the dentist. He arranged for me to pay the rest a little bit at a time. He patched up my tooth and fastened some wires to two other teeth. After a while the wires caused the two teeth to go bad. Then I had to have some more work done. Eventually I had to have a bridge that I wore the rest of my life. One time I was going on a short trip. A few days before leaving, I decided to have a candy bar. The bar had been in the store refrigerator and was hard as a rock. I bit into that candy bar and out came my bridge. This was just before the Fourth of July. I was lucky to have such a nice dentist. He and his wife worked over the holiday, fixed my bridge and got me ready to look presentable on my trip.

One of my freshman classmates was a kid named Ralph Neves. He was a Portuguese kid, good looking but he was very cocky. His whole life was wrapped up in horses. He was always skipping school and running off to the race track. They just couldn't keep him in school. Finally I guess the school gave up on him. He eventually became a very famous jockey. He was very well known because he won so many races. At the race track he was nicknamed "The Portuguese Pepper-Pot". In the year of 1936, at a Bay Meadows horse race, his mount threw him into a wooden rail. He fell off of his mount and was seriously trampled. In fact, he was declared dead by the track doctor. An ambulance took him to the morgue. At the morgue, the doctor in attendance was a friend of Neves. Just taking a chance that Neves might be revived, he gave him a shot of adrenaline into the heart. Nothing happened, Neves was dead, so the doctor locked up the facility and left. In about fifteen minutes Neves revived, dressed and took a taxi back to the track. When his wife, who was still in her box seat, saw him walk back on the track, she fainted. He wanted to race again that same afternoon, but the officials refused to let him ride until the next day. This hard to believe tale just happens to be a true story.

Because "The Mob" was so powerful at the racetrack, often they would try to get the jockeys to throw a race. Neves wanted no part of that game. He hired a bodyguard because it wasn't unheard of, for a jockey to get his legs broken or worse, for not going along with the gangsters. Neves and his bodyguard certainly looked like the "Odd Couple". To see little short Neves walking down the street with his over six foot bodyguard was a quite a sight. Neves was eventually inducted into the National Racing Hall of Fame as well as the Washington Racing Hall of Fame.

There was a nice teacher in high school that took an interest in me. It bothered her that my crossed eye had never been corrected. She asked me if I would like to have it straightened. Of course I wanted my eyes to look normal but, I didn't have any money for such an expensive operation. My teacher said she would look into it for me. First she took me to the Community Health Center. After the initial examination, she took me into San Francisco to Green's Eye Hospital. They did the repair with no charge. My eye had been crossed for so many years; it was too late to preserve much of the sight. Even so, I was thankful for the improved appearance. I was very grateful for this nice teacher who was instrumental in getting my eye straightened.

There was one time while we were in "The Willows" that was a little frightening. My brother and I had gone to bed and were sound asleep. It was sometime in the middle of the night, when a racket outside woke us up. All at once there was all of this pounding on our door. There was no lock, but we had secured the door with a two by four bar across it. Anyone would have had a hard time breaking in. "Help, help, help me, let me in." this scary voice was yelling and screaming while the pounding went on. My brother and I never made a sound. Naturally I was petrified. The racket went on for a few minutes then it abruptly stopped. We stayed as quiet as two little mice for a long time. After a while, I guess whoever it was, thought no one was home so they went away. We were lucky they didn't try to force that rickety door open. That was the only time in all those years we lived in "The Willows" that anyone ever tried to bother us.

By the time Carl was in the tenth grade, I was often by myself. My brother was very gregarious, so he had a lot of friends. They would invite him to stay at their homes. He wasn't the least bit bashful. Their homes were a lot better than where we lived, so he was gone a lot. After a while about the only time I saw him was at school. He became friends with a kid named Kenny. I guess Carl stayed with him most of the time. While still in school he got a job at an art studio. He worked there for several months. There came a time when I no longer saw my brother at school. I didn't know what had happened to him. Later I found out that he had moved and was going to school in Burlingame. He never let me know, even when he graduated from high school. Many months passed before he finally got in touch with me. When World War II was declared, Carl got a job in a defense plant, so he was exempted from active duty. Toward the end of the war he was finally drafted. After a short while, he was medically discharged because of his health.

Carl was a lady's man from a very early age. He always had lots of girl friends. He met a family by the name of McDaniels. They had a big house over by the railroad depot. He became friends with the family and eventually married Virginia, one of the McDaniels' girls. Little did I know then that this family was going to have a great impact on my life but that is a story for another time. This marriage of my brother's didn't last. He was married several times.

I can say one thing about my brother, he was very talented. He learned to fly, taught skiing, he was a great golfer, a super dancer and a wonderful artist. From the time he was a teenager, he more or less went his own way. It seemed to me that my brother was always searching for something, but never found it. Growing up he was always forceful and bold. He was positive where I was negative. He was forever lending me a hand when we were young. Actually, I looked up to him, even though he was younger than I.

When I finally realized that I was really by myself, I was too busy to be lonely. When school was out for the day, and by the time I walked six miles home. there wasn't much time to fool around. I had to take time to shop for groceries nearly every evening, and then cook my meal. There were studies every night. Sometimes when I went into the grocery store, the owner would ask, "Son what are you fixing for your supper tonight?"

No matter what answer I would give, he might say, "Why don't you stay here and eat with my wife and me?" That pleased me because his wife was a good cook.

The train track was very close to where we built our little shack. One weekend I didn't have anything else to do, so I decided to go for a ride. When the train slowed down, I hopped on a car that was carrying gravel from South San Francisco into the city. In a few days I happened to see my dentist. He scolded me, "I saw you sitting on that freight train. What did you think you were doing?"

"Oh I was just taking a ride." That was a lot of fun. I have no idea how I ever got home from San Francisco.

During the depression, when Roosevelt was president, there were a lot of agencies established for the unemployed to earn money. There was the WPA, SERA, and a program for students whose families had a low income. One of my teachers arranged a job for me under this program. The job was to clean the school typewriters. After the typing classes were over, I went in and gave all of the machines a good going over. The pay really wasn't much, but to me it was a fortune.

One time my dad came up from the desert to see how we were getting along. He asked if I needed anything. I told him that I didn't especially need anything, but I sure would like to have a radio. He went right out and bought me a little white one. I really loved that radio. Every chance I had, I listened to the talk shows that told you how to eat to be healthy. Right then I began to pay attention to my meals. I made sure I had lots of vegetables and fruit. I would buy the little bitty cans of food so I wouldn't have any leftovers. I fried potatoes or made pancakes from "scratch" for my breakfast. I never cooked oatmeal or had cereal because I would have had to use canned milk. I couldn't stand that stuff. I kept everything cleaned up so I never had any ants.

One day, my friend from school, Frank Turner, wanted to come home with me. He thought the way I lived was "neat". While he was there, I fried us some potatoes. "Those are the best potatoes I've ever had," he bragged. "I wish my mother could fry potatoes like these."

I especially liked gym. I wasn't much of an athlete, but the gym class gave me a chance to shower every day. That was a lot easier than carrying water, heating enough for a bath and then bathing in a wash tub. I was always clean but a daily shower was great. Once when I was much younger I didn't wash my neck good enough. My father beat me and blacked both my eyes. I know he was sorry afterward, but he just lost his temper. That was the only time he ever hit me.

High School went pretty fast even if I did have to spend that extra year as a freshman. Before I knew it, I was a senior. I never dated. In the first place I was still too shy. In fact I was afraid of girls. My brother was just the opposite. He was like my dad. Every time they turned around they had a new girl friend. The second reason I didn't date was that I just didn't have the money for socializing. I barely had enough to exist. My brother was more worldly wise than I. Even though I had read and heard about what happened between males and females, it was hard for me to believe that those nice girls would do anything like "THAT".

One time I heard that Sally Rand, the famous fan dancer, was going to be in San Francisco. Boy, oh boy! I was finally going to be able to see "something". I hoarded my money so I would be able to have the admission price as well as streetcar fare there and back. I was so excited I could hardly stand it. I heard that she didn't have a stitch of clothes on behind those fans. When she switched those fans around, I was finally going to be able to get down to the nitty-gritty and see the whole "thing". Finally I was in the theater. The show started and I'm on the edge of my seat. The curtains parted and out came Sally Rand. The audience applauded. The hair stood up on the back of my neck. When the music started, there she was dancing around on the stage, flipping those fans back and forth, like the speed of light. She moved those fans so fast you couldn't see anything. What a disappointment! I spent all of that money and all I saw was a bunch of feathers.

I had one teacher who realized I didn't live with a family. I don't know how she found out because very few people knew I lived alone. I was surprised when one day she told me, "After school, I want you to come in to see me. I have something for you." I couldn't imagine what in the world she could have for me. When I got to her room she was smiling. "I thought you might like something special for your supper, so I baked you a cake." What a nice surprise! As I look back over those difficult years, I was fortunate in many ways. I got to know a lot of caring, generous people, especially my teachers.

When it was time for graduation, my dad came up from the desert to see me. This is just the second time I had seen him in four years. I didn't have any clothes that were fit for this special occasion. One day we were with one of his friends, Dad had recognized that I needed something better to wear. Naturally he decided we would go down to the Goodwill and get me a suit. His friend spoke up, scolding, "Joe, this is your oldest son and the first to graduate. Graduation is a special time for a young person. Come on man, he needs something nice. Why don't you get the kid a new suit for once in his life?" My dad thought for a minute, mulling over what his friend had told him. Finally he looked at me and grinned, "Come on son, let's go shopping for graduation clothes." That was one happy day for me. My dad didn't stick around for graduation night. One of my teachers asked how I was going to get to the auditorium. I told her I guess I would have to walk. She said that six miles was just too far, especially at night. She arranged to meet me somewhere close to my place. She would drive me to the graduation exercises and back again. Once more one of my wonderful, caring teachers came to my rescue. I attended my high school graduation alone. No family was there to witness my accomplishment.

This was the year of 1936. It was not only the year of my graduation, but also the year of other major events in the country. This was the year that the United States Government mailed out the first Social Security checks. In California, finally completed, the Oakland Bay Bridge was at last opened.

Chapter 11

I was determined to go on to college. One of my teachers advised me to go to a junior college instead of trying for a four-year college. At that time, junior colleges were a part of the secondary education program. There was no tuition; however I would have to buy my books and supplies. A student card would cost four dollars but you really weren't forced to buy that. For a young man in my position, on his own and very little money, it seemed the logical solution. I enrolled into San Mateo Junior College. That was the closest junior college to where I lived, but still about forty miles away. I had to take the streetcar and it cost ten cents each way. Money was hard to come by, so there was seldom any left over for clothes or any other extras.

I never knew anything about advisers therefore I made up my own course of study. I looked over the courses available and enrolled in those I thought would be interesting. I signed up for trigonometry, descriptive geometry, geology, surveying, hygiene and gym. That was a killer course as I soon found out.

Curtis wearing blue sweater with white S Won for
playing Soccer at San Mateo Junior College

I had just one white shirt, so every day that had to be washed, dried and ironed. Everyone at that time wore dirty cords. That was the style, so I didn't have to worry about those. I had that long streetcar ride, had to buy food and cook, besides studying. Sometimes I had time to go to study hall and study at school. We had no lockers, so I had to carry all of my books with me. In P.E., I went out for soccer. When I dressed out for gym, the rest of the kids made fun of me because I wore bathing trunks for underwear. It didn't take very long for me to realize that I was in over my head. By the time I muddled through the first semester, I could see that continuing was a lost cause. Even though there was no tuition, I just didn't have the money to carry on, so I dropped out. However, I came away with a letter in soccer. I had earned the right to a beautiful dark blue sweater with a big white "S" on the pocket.

I loved school. Leaving it was a great disappointment for me, because I wanted a college education more than anything I could think of. It would be many years before that dream would finally come true. In the meantime, I had to find a way to support myself. I talked to my high school mechanical drawing teacher. He said he thought he could help me find a decent job. He knew of several places that were hiring. He took me first to U.S. Steel Company. They had an opening in their testing laboratory. It would have been a great job but I just didn't know enough. Next we went over to Western Pipe and Steel. Here a person had to work around a lot of machinery. With my poor eyesight, they were afraid to hire me. Finally we went to Lindy Air Products. They made a lot of things like oxygen, hydrogen and a bunch of other chemicals. This company had an opening in the office. They hired me at four dollars a day. That was great. Now that I had a job it was time to change my way of living. As soon as I saved up a little nest egg, I rented a room in a boarding house. I then packed up my meager amount of clothes and gathered together what few personal things I had managed to accumulate. I walked out of that little shack in "The Willows" leaving everything else behind. I closed the door, walked away and never looked back.

It was sixty-five years later that I realized my dream of going to college. I was living in Red Bluff and was retired. I decided it was now or never. I went to Shasta Junior College to enroll. The first thing they did was to put me in front of a computer. I didn't know a mouse from a rat. The girls in charge said they weren't supposed to help me, but I think they felt sorry for this poor old man. They saw to it that all of the preliminary paper work was done correctly. Next, I went to see an advisor. This time the course of study they suggested was more reasonable. Since I wasn't in pursuit of a career, they said a general education course would be best for me. I agreed and enrolled in the required courses for the first semester. One difficult thing was using the computer. Use a computer; I couldn't even type! I had to learn and learn fast. I can tell you, that at my age, studying was not all that easy. I am glad that all of my life I had been an avid reader. That was a big help. There were all of those reports and term papers that were required. I had never done a lot of writing, and had no idea how to write a term paper. With a lot of help and advice from the faculty as well as some of the students, somehow I made it. This time there was no quitting. Two years later I graduated with honors from Shasta Junior College, in Redding, California. I was one of over three-hundred graduates. This time, a host of friends and family were there to wish me well.

Graduating at the age of eighty-six, I was the oldest graduate Shasta College had ever had!

Now that I am past ninety years old, I look back and find that there were some good times and some that were not so good. I have had more experiences in one lifetime than most people could ever imagine having. I am not through yet. There are many more books to read, many more places to see, and a lot more to experience. I am looking forward to the rest of the years allotted to me. I may not have been born until I was eight years old, but once I got started, there was no stopping me.

Curtis Graduation
Shasta Junior College 2003

Use with permission by Record Searchlight Newspaper.

About the Author

Gwyndolin Teney- Rangell

Gwyndolin Teney-Rangell has lived most of her ninety-four years in Northern California. She received a B.A. from Chico State University in Elementary Education. She enjoyed her many years of teaching and later as a Real Estate Broker. She now lives alone and enjoys reading, gardening, traveling and her many friends.

Printed in the United States
By Bookmasters